This is why you prepare for college is the college preparatory book as part of the THIS IS WHY series. I am here to prepare you for success in college by ensuring you make the right choice for YOU while in high school. Understand that there are things you can control leading up to which college you choose. You will be better prepared socially, mentally and physically for your journey of higher education inside and outside the classroom after reading this. What you learn in the classroom in high school is important and you need to work hard to achieve the grades as apart of the process but while you are being the best person you can be in class you also need to do your part outside the classroom.

"There is more to college than just going to class."

Part of the THIS IS WHY series

www.thisiswhydoc.com

J. YANCY MERCHANT JR

THIS IS WHY YOU PREPARE FOR COLLEGE

Copyright 2019 by James Yancy Merchant New Face Management, LLC

All rights reserved.

This book or any portion thereof may not be reproduced or used in any manner whatsoever with the express written permission of the publisher except for the use of brief quotations in a book review or scholarly Journal

This publication is designed to provide accurate and authoritative information in regard to the subject matter covered. It is sold with the understanding that the publisher is not engaged in rendering legal, accounting or other professional service. If legal advice or other expert assistance is required, the services of a competent professional person should be sought-from a declaration of principles jointly adapted by a committee of the American Bar Association and a committee of publishers association.

All brand names and product names used in this book

are trademarks, registered trademarks or trade names of their respective holders. New Face Management, LLC is not associated with any product or vendor in this book.

First printing 2019

copyright.gov

9781693909214Paperback ISBN

Published by James Yancy Merchant Jr

New Face Management, LLC

Success Without Limitations, Inc.

www.thisiswhydoc.com

Cover design by

Khaleel Artis, J. Yancy Merchant and Ralph Oliver

Editing by

Dr. Kenya Malcolm, Angee Costa, Jessica Washington, Candyce Payton

Worksheets by

Taylor Gribble, Deon Haraway and J. Yancy Merchant

Illustration by Geryn Harris

This book is dedicated to all high school students who are looking for direction to be successful in life

"Fingers interlocked ...not one child left behind"

REVIEWS :

This text is a motivator for experiential learning and what it means to mentally and emotionally prepare for an experience that will intrinsically develop incoming students and their supporters pre-college.

Coupled with shared personal stories and a communal voice, "This Is Why You Prepare for College" fosters the idea that true success stretches beyond first selecting a major and instead illuminates the difference between interest and passion, self-assesses mental capacity, leans into the significance of serviceable connections, draws upon the power of healthy circles, and showcases how to maximize resources.

The rationale for its content is clear and gives permission to curiosities embedded in the preparation process. Every consideration, to best prepare for a journey of scholarship, spans the lines of these pages. I recommend this text for education practitioners, deans, high school counselors, administrators, stakeholders, community members, adult learners, returning students, and parents.

James Yancy Merchant set out to create a learning tool and I'd consider this a job well done.

-Jovan Brown, School Leader and Writer in Brooklyn, NY

"This is Why You Prepare For College by J. Yancy Merchant, Jr serves as a road map for high school students. Through the

authors detailed examples and resources he provides the necessities students need to be successful during their college years. Furthermore, he breakdowns each step from beginning to end so that students are prepared. Merchant primary goal is for students is to go into college debt free, ultimately being ready and staying ahead of the game."

– Taylor Gribble undergraduate student at Central Michigan University

"This book puts you ahead of everyone else and on the right path towards all of your career goals in the future. This Is Why is definitely a must read, I repeat this book is a must read! You can take this book throughout your high school years then be set and ready for the smoothest transition possible going into college. After you finish "This Is Why you prepare for college" I highly recommend you to go and purchase "This Is Why you go to college," it will put you above and beyond where you feel you'll be, going into higher education."

-Deon Haraway, Hampton University Class of 2019 Business Administration Major

"This is Why you prepare for college by Mr. Yancy Merchant Jr., truly what every high school student needs. This book gives the best information possible for the moving forward into future. The advice he gives is real and raw, he keeps it completely 100. When using this book, high school students will be way ahead of their peers. I wish I had this book when I was in high school, it would have made the transition into college so much easier. Merchant *breaks down every detail from registering for testing to walking across the stage for graduation. It is a MUST read."*

-Marli Peters Sophomore Strategic Communications major

ABOUT THE AUTHOR

James Yancy Merchant, Jr.is the owner of New Face Management, Llc and creator of Success Without Limitations, Inc.

Originally from Queens, New York, Yancy was a scholar student and talented athlete. His childhood and adolescent years would provide a series of opportunities to gain interest in both the business and event planning industry. Upon graduation from high school, he and best friend Sean Washington committed to attending a historically black college noting its prominence in academia and culture would introduce these young men to a new world of possibilities. Both young men were accepted into the prestigious institution of Hampton University with the intention of developing into young, successful entrepreneurs within the Hampton Roads area. As thriving, full-time students in exceptional academic standing, Merchant and Washington soon befriended fellow scholar Dr. Howard Crumpton and the three would establish the promotional company Straight face Entertainment at eighteen years old. Later Mr. Merchant became the sole owner of the company known as New Face Entertainment, Inc. by twenty-two all while graduating cum laude with a bachelor degree in business management in four years.

New Face became more than a profitable company; it evolved into a movement. As their network increased in size and quality, New Face hosted more than on and off campus events. As a company, New Face empowered college students and alumni socially, professionally, emotionally and mentally. New Face provided over $10,000 in scholarships and donations towards student organizations, created numerous internship opportunities for students in their respective fields, sponsored athletic events, hosted mental health seminars, initiated beautification projects, offered tutoring services, donated food and clothing to homeless shelters and so much more.

While managing New Face, Merchant created the community-based component of the company, Success Without Limitations. Presently, he is expanding SWL, rebranded now known as New Face to New Face Management, LLC doing management consulting. He is also the creator, director, and producer of This is Why, a series documenting a historical reflection of college life outside the classroom and beyond set to release in 2019. Merchant is also a proud father. He works for the city of New York and is developing a series of memoirs on the breadth, journey, and lessons learned from his life and experience in the entertainment business. New Face prior members, interns and employees have given their knowledge to assist with the THIS IS WHY series. Learn from the successes but most importantly hear the stories and advice written in this book and learn from our failures to be better than us in life. THIS IS WHY YOU PREPARE FOR COLLEGE.

LET'S CONNECT!

For information on special sales, workshops, networking, leadership speaking events, tutoring sessions contact me below:

- www.thisiswhydoc.com
- Yancy@newfacemanagement.org
- https://twitter.com/newfaceceo
- https://instagram.com/THISISWHYDOC
- https://www.facebook.com/newfaceceo/

Also be sure to youtube and search @newfaceceo to view documentary interviews of all college alumni who assisted in this series!

College Tours

As a part of the **Success Without Limitations** Initiative,

We will be providing college tours for High School Students.

For more information view www.newfacemangement.org and click on Success Without Limitations.

Feel free to email SWLINC05@gmail.com for more information.

"Fingers interlocked ...not one child left behind"

Apply now for the Annual Success Without Limitations Scholarship

Email <u>SWLinc05@gmail.com</u> for more information on applying and donating to the fund

PREFACE

The easy part is reading the book. The hard part is applying everything in the book to your everyday life. Trust me, it can be done. This is just the beginning as a student in high school. The people mentioned in this book are living proof that college is critical to your success. It's not what you learn in class in college but what you learn outside the classroom. Please visit www.thisiswhydoc.com to watch the stories of all the stories of the college students mentioned in this book. Benefit from hearing our experiences.

TABLE OF CONTENTS

Purpose 1

INTRODUCTION 3

Inspirational Person Dr. Howard Crumpton, Phd 6

Invest in yourself 8

The 10,000 hours 11

PAY FOR COLLEGE BEFORE YOU GRADUATE 17

Inspirational Person Sean Washington 18

PAY FOR COLLEGE BEFORE YOU GRADUATE 21

THE DECISION THAT WILL CHANGE YOUR LIFE 38

INSPIRATIONAL PERSON Day'nah Cooper-Evans 39

Building character leaders not just successful leaders 87

INSPIRATIONAL PERSON Ashley Company 89

Inspirational person Victor Rogers 91

Karmia Berry, Founder of IAMCULTURED 113

Dominique Wilkins, Co founder of SHEChicago 116

J. Yancy Merchant, Jr creator Success Without Limitations 119

Community Service 121

Be a Mentor 123

Inspirational Person Justin Sharpe 125

Mental Health 126

Steps to preventing a potential suicide 133

Resources for help: 136

This is far from over … 141

SUGGESTED READING MATERIAL AND REFERENCES 142

Why a book series? 146

About New Face Management, LLC 152

THIS IS WHY DOCUMENTARY 154

Afterword 156

PURPOSE

The purpose of this book series is twofold: to prepare future college students for life-changing events and to give actual real-life examples of people who have vast amounts of generationally relatable experiences. In other words, we have been there and done what new students are preparing to accomplish.

One of my mottos is "Learn from me... learn from us." It is a principle I have always taught from experience rather than theory. Even before becoming a teacher, I found practical application to be an effective way to convey essential concepts to high school and college students. Mentors can use this guide to teach youth the right path to be successful in all of their endeavors.

Each section begins with a "Person of Inspiration" or a "Featured Business." Each person or business is a part of my network and the *This Is Why* documentary. They are examples of people who went to college and were successful outside of the classroom, which ultimately helped them excel in their careers. Each of these people, though not all famous, is an inspiration because of their dedication which has led to their success. Each section also features quotes and advice from different college graduates. They took the time to add their perspectives to help make this publication as powerful as possible. It's important to hear about successful people from the community who aren't on the TV screen.

I want you to read this book to learn, of course. But, I also want to inspire you to teach and spread this knowledge to as many people as possible. I want this to serve as a learning tool for young adults. I didn't write this series to be a one-time read. It is meant to be a continuous resource for college students, high school students, and teachers of LIFE.

INTRODUCTION

If I told you, you don't go to college to sit in a classroom and learn the same things you learn in high school over again, would you believe me?

If I told you, when you go away to college you will learn more in the first four months about yourself than you did all four years in high school, would you believe me ?

I wrote this book after I wrote **THIS IS WHY** *you go to college* to give college students the keys to success. After the book was completed and listening to people in my network who helped make this whole project happen, I realized that it if I was able to line up high school students with similar tools early they will be able to achieve even greater success in college and be better prepared for my methods. I will go over all of these in this book giving different nuggets to prepare you for college leading up to my New Face Method of Success in **THIS IS WHY** you go to college: How to successfully graduate in REAL LIFE Studies.

This is how you prepare for college is a learning mechanism that walks you through various parts of the college preparation process that you may not learn from a guidance counselor or in the classroom.

Going to college for class is only half of what you learn and if you think about the actual skills you develop in the four plus years while away for college, the classroom knowledge gained in comparison to what you learn outside the classroom is even less than that. The knowledge and experience gained outside of the classroom is unmatched but it all starts with how prepared for college you are in high school.

There are certain things you need to do in high school before you get to college in order to set yourself up for the most success possible in college and surviving as a young adult.

Most books you read about college preparedness will focus on getting good grades and the application process. I am here to prepare you for success in college by ensuring you make the right choice for YOU while in high school and understanding that there are things you can control leading up to which college you choose and being socially, mentally, and physically prepared for your journey of higher education in and outside the classroom. What you learn in the classroom in high school is important and you need to work hard to achieve the grades as a part of the process but while you are being the best person you can be in class you also need to do your part outside the classroom.

In *THIS IS WHY you prepare for college* some of the topics include:

- Researching scholarships and grants to have your education paid for
- Choosing the right college for you
- Time Management
- Being and leader and exemplifying strong characteristics

- Networking

- Mental health awareness

Throughout this journey, I will ask you questions for you to think about and discuss with others you know who are going to college. I will give you examples of current students and alumni who have already walked the path and have wisdom to share. They took the time to add their perspectives to help make this publication as powerful as possible. It's important to hear about successful people from the community anyone can relate to.

For the adult-motivators reading this who may be looking for answers to give others, I want you to think about your life and explore new and innovative ways to advise students. I encourage you to think about how it felt to be a teenager and how you would have liked to be helped with the important decisions teenagers have to make.

For teenagers thinking about college or already in college, I want you to open your eyes and see the potential of greatness ahead of you. The world is yours to conquer and this book will add tools for you to use to build your world.

INSPIRATIONAL PERSON
Dr. Howard Crumpton, Phd

Howard Crumpton, PhD is the owner and CEO of Reach Out Therapy, LLC. Dr. Crumpton earned his Ph.D. in Clinical Psychology from the Curry School of Education at the University of Virginia. His clinical internship, with specialties rotations in Adolescent Medicine and Bilingual Assessment, was completed at Children's Hospital Los Angeles, a part of the University of Southern California University Center for Excellence in Developmental Disabilities.

Upon completion of his doctoral degree, Dr. Crumpton spent two years as a postdoctoral fellow at the Kennedy Krieger Institute within the Johns Hopkins University School of Medicine in Maryland. There, he trained in the Behavior Management and Child and Family Therapy clinics, providing multi-systemic support to parents, medical professionals, and educators in addressing emotional, behavioral, social, and academic problems in children and adolescents. Dr. Crumpton served as a Spanish-English bilingual staff psychologist and key contributor to the development of the Primary Care Behavioral Health Services at the Children's National Health System, where he provided family focused therapy, assessment and behavioral health consultations in collaboration with medical professionals within and outside the hospital system. He has also served as a psychological evaluator at The MECCA Group, LLC, a private practice in Washington, DC owned and operated by women of color. Dr. Crumpton currently provides mental health and consultative services for families as a family psychologist at Encore Recovery Services in Arlington, VA, a substance recovery startup that provides young adults and their families with holistic cutting-edge services to address substance addiction and co-occurring mental health disorders.

While Dr. Crumpton's target population includes all children, he holds particular interests in treating such concerns in the Latino community with families whose primary language is Spanish. His demonstrated research interests include increasing motivation and academic success of low-achieving students, the impact of warm and supportive teacher-student interactions on student classroom behavior, and the psychological assessment of culturally and linguistically diverse student populations.

Dr. Crumpton currently resides in the Washington, DC area with his wife and three children. In his spare time, Dr. Crumpton plays the drums, learns new languages, travels with his family, and plays video games.

INVEST IN YOURSELF

I have reflected on my time as a young adult and realized that, although many of the choices I made then didn't seem critical at the time, it turned out to be some of the most life-changing decisions I've ever make. Young people are told by parents and other influential adults tell that college is the natural next step after high school. What is college? Is it supposed to be the 13-16th grades? Or is it a place we went just to leave the house where we grew up?

In a four-year institution, typically students are working on a Bachelor's degree. During that time, you are referred to as an undergraduate student – *undergrad* for short. As an undergrad, I wanted to be successful in everything I did. From my freshman year, I was active in multiple organizations. I wanted to touch every part of campus possible. The set up for success starts early. Have fun, but get active. Even as a freshman, my first year, I started a business with my best friends called Straight Face/New Face Entertainment. Whenever we did anything as the owners of our event planning company, it doesn't feel like a job. It's just fun!

For the student who hates going to classes and/or isn't the best test taker, college could seem like nothing more than four more years of more exams, teachers, and grades. College students know that it is so much more. But how do prospective students get a handle on what college life is like? How would they know that college literally changes your life the minute you move away from your comfortable hometown and step foot on that college campus with bags in your hand into a dorm room? College is certainly not a second high school experience. It is so much more.

College opens opportunities you would never have if you stay in the same place you were in the 12th grade. College gives you the chance to meet people from places you have never been. They are confused and excited at the same time about being away from home.

College is an investment in yourself. You have to understand that there is no way you will be successful if you don't invest in your personal growth. College is a big step in this growth in a number of ways. It is where you gain independence while continuing to invest in your own education. While learning and developing people skills, college is where you learn to fail and get back up. It's about survival of the fittest. In order to succeed you have to go through struggles and experience things on your own. College is the time and age where you can do that while investing in yourself in a positive way and still being surrounded with people with similar goals from all walks of life. High School is the time you use to prepare for that next step. Even as a teenager 13-18 you have to utilize that time to prepare for that next step as a college student. Time management is very important. I want you to enjoy life as a teenager. I want you to have fun and be a teen. You can still enjoy yourself and prepare for your future. Think about what you like to do and see how you can turn that into something that can become a mechanism to either pay for college or set you up for a successful future. That is what the majority of your time needs to be spent on.

THE 10,000 HOURS

"Use what you got to get what you want"

On average, people waste about 4-6 hours a day. That's 28-42 hours a week, 112-168 hours a month, 1,344-2,016 hours a year. Imagine what you could've created if you had used that 2,000 hours! High School is filled with classes, sports and different organizations and some of you may even have a part time job. Being able to balance organizations, classes, homework, and fun is essential. It sounds like a lot but can all be done with proper planning. When people ask me how I balance my days and planning, I say all the time, "I have the same 24 hours as Diddy."

I was told a long time ago that it takes about 10,000 hours to master a skill combined with talent. Breaking that down in years, you must practice for six to ten years to get great depending on how often you do it and how dedicated you are. That's why I instill in all my children and my mentees to get better daily. If you want to do something, DO IT and be great at it, especially if you have already found your talent. You can learn the skill.

In high school, I played varsity basketball and was a captain on my team. I also played football and ran track but was not skilled enough to play college sports. By 11th grade I held class offices, was a part of multiple organizations and had a part time job but I didn't have someone pushing me to pursue sports at a young age to think that I could actually work on that skill and craft to have a sport of a craft pay for my education.

Deon Merritt who is the owner of Real Skills, a High intensity skills program in Queens, New York, went to St. Raymond high school in the Bronx, NY and played college Division 1 basketball for the University of Richmond and South Alabama University. He spends time in the community encouraging kids to get better and work hard to achieve their goals. He tells his players that basketball can be a ticket to a free education if you work hard. He encourages them to utilize the tools they've been given and use them to their advantage. I have a son, LJ (James Yancy Merchant III) who wants to play basketball. He's ten years old now and Deon trains him consistently.

If you are not the best test taker and your family doesn't have all the money in the world, playing sports and excelling by working on your craft is an option that can put you in a position to get that college experience and education for free. Once you get to college, you will be a part of a team that will keep you focused and on task to be successful. Not everyone will become a professional sports player, but you can use sports to pay for your education to do other things in life. Even if your goal is to become a sports agent, a coach, a doctor, own your own business... sports can help pay for your education. The best things is — you will graduate with zero student loan debt placing you one step ahead of a student who didn't play sports and just went to class. It's not easy though. It takes hard work and dedication.

Now, let's take a look at the 10,000 hours along with Mr. Merritt's story and apply it to sports, as an example. People with "natural talent" in basketball still need to put in 10,000 hours of work developing their skills. So, whether you are talking about typing, learning how to run a business, practicing law, medicine, or becoming a world-renowned DJ, even someone who is a "natural talent" puts in those hours to be great.

Round that 2.7 hours a day to three hours. So, a ten year old who wants to be a "master" by the time he is twenty should expect to work on playing the sport three hours a day every day for ten years. Sound crazy? It doesn't sound crazy to me at all. Keep in mind if you aren't willing to have this kind of dedication don't expect to be considered "a master" or good enough to be a professional or even receive a free education. You have to be realistic. A productive three hours of daily learning will help you excel in anything. Of course, you will need a great teacher/mentor to teach the skills needed so that you are learning the right way to do things. For example, you can't have a football coach teaching you how to play basketball. There are different ways to learn as well. It's not just physically playing a sport. It's researching, reading, learning, and understanding the craft.

How much time did you spend in school learning how to read and write? You were taught these things that eventually became second nature. As you continued to learn about reading and writing, you were able to add to your skills. The same applies to sports or anything craft in which you hope to excel. First, you learn the basics, then you add to it, and then you learn, practice, learn, practice and learn some more. You can adjust the numbers to your specific goals; increase or decrease the hours as age and time allows. But never neglect practice and learning. Nothing is life is given to you. It's earned. Remember that working and playing hard means you need to add in time for rest and recovery.

A major component to my method for success is planning and having goals. Keeping in mind that it takes roughly 10,000 hours to become a "master of a craft," you now know you have to dedicate yourself by staking the time every day to learn and get better at what you want your craft to be. How does knowing this change the timeline for your goals? Does it change your commitment? Remember, that sports are just an example and a common way that some people are able to get their education paid for but you can work on being the master of any craft YOU want.

I recommend using the gifts and tools you were born with to pay for your education. You've been developing your talents with hard work; do your due diligence to apply for athletic and academic scholarships. Showcase your talents on the court or field or by competing on academic teams to have the best opportunity to get your education paid for by doing what you do best. Find the university that best fits your talents and skills that will pay for you to get a degree doing what comes natural. Academically, your goal — at a MINIMUM – is to have a 3.0 Grade Point Average (GPA) in high school.

High School is a prime time to develop your mental muscle. Your ability to learn will set you up for college success. Even if you play sports, you have to prepare yourself academically to get the best free education possible. If you don't play sports, there are a number of different options for scholarships. I'll share several of them throughout, but you have to do your part academically to get as many offers possible. Many people don't realize that many schools will pay for your education in exchange for your extracurricular performance. Many women in my family danced at DeVore Dance Center owned and operated by Carolyn Devore in Queens, NY. For as long as I can remember, my sisters, my cousins, and my aunts have been involved with Devore. There are young women and men who graduate every year from High School and Devore Dance. Often, they can use that time and talent in dance to acquire scholarships in exchange for their participation in various University dance programs that offer that free education. You have to go out and research which colleges offer scholarships in your extra curricular field.

I advise people who play a sport or are involved in performing arts have someone record your games or recitals so that you have footage to send to various schools. This is a visual highlight that showcases your talents. Get familiar with video editing programs like Final cut pro and iMovie. Use outlets like YouTube, Facebook, and Instagram to display your talents. Practice using those editing programs while in high school so that you become proficient with them. Editing footage could also be a source of income to help pay for necessities while in high school and college. Computer Science is a major that you may want to consider if editing is something you begin to become proficient in as well. Schools need your talents and may be willing to waive some or all of your tuition. If you dance or play an instrument, there is a school that will pay for you to do what you love every day in exchange for a college education. Most applications and colleges have deadlines, which means you have to do your research and get organized. Don't think that offers to pay for your schooling are going to just fall in your lap. No matter what you heard, it doesn't happen that way. You have to do your research to find out what schools offer scholarships and what organizations will sponsor you. Start as early as the 9th grade researching scholarship opportunities. Trust me when I tell you, there are students right now getting scholarships and grants you deserve to have but need to go out and get it.

PAY FOR COLLEGE BEFORE YOU GRADUATE

INSPIRATIONAL PERSON Sean Washington

FAFSA

ESSAYS

Band scholarships

Sports scholarships

Academic scholarships

The best Advice I can give

Suggested scholarship links

Suggested reading material

Take home Messages

INSPIRATIONAL PERSON
Sean Washington

Sean Washington is a results-oriented business professional who excels in attracting, retaining, deepening and developing business relationships. As a Senior Business Development Manager in the Economic Development Department in the city of Norfolk, Virginia, Sean is responsible for the administration of capital access programs that assist with the start-up, growth, and expansion of businesses in the City of Norfolk. Sean also serves as the Assistant Executive Director and Secretary/Treasurer for the Economic Development Authority for the City of Norfolk.

Raised in Long Island, New York, Sean became a member of the Hampton Roads community as a Business Administration student at Hampton University. During his undergraduate tenure, he served as president of the New York Pre-Alumni Association and the Entrepreneurship Club. He was also a member of the OFVC Entrepreneurship Invitational Business Plan Team and The Society of Business Professionals. His entrepreneurial spirit led to the co-creation of the promotional company "New Face Entertainment," which created a lasting mark on campus activities.

Sean began his professional career as a financial representative for American General Finance, a subsidiary of AIG. There, he had the responsibility of personal and real estate lending, monitoring delinquent accounts and proposing financing options to retail dealers. His efforts not only raised the branch's overall lending volume from $14 to $15 million, but a 10% profit gain was recognized from 2007-2008. In 2011, Sean expanded his finance and lending experience by being selected into the BB&T Leadership Development Program, which resulted in his previous title of Assistant Vice President at BB&T Bank. As a small business lender and market leader, Sean was responsible for managing a $34.5 million deposit portfolio and a $15 million lending portfolio.

Sean balances his passion for helping small businesses thrive while giving countless hours of his time to the community. He's a board member of Parents Against Bullying VA, previously served as president of the Urban League of Hampton Roads Young Professionals, and was co-chair for BB&T's Multicultural Committee during his tenure with the bank. Sean has also volunteered with the Cystic Fibrosis Foundation, Roc Solid Organization,

I-THRive mentoring program, Toastmasters International, and Norfolk's Bank-on Your Success Program, where he assists individuals and families reach their financial goals. He is also the Assistant Department Head of the Sound Ministry at Full Gospel Kingdom Church. Sean spends his downtime reading, exercising, and traveling with his wife, Jessica Larche Washington.

One of Sean's favorite quotes is

"Don't let your charisma take you somewhere your character can't keep you."

Sean's integrity, hard work and faithfulness to both his career and community are evidence of his highly respected character. He looks forward to building a legacy of service and growth for years to come.

PAY FOR COLLEGE BEFORE YOU GRADUATE

Once of your primary objectives is to determine how you will pay for your college education. Based on the experience of myself and my peers, having your college education paid for before you graduate puts you ahead of the game since you won't start your post-college life worried about debt. Most people expect to go to college, obtain their degrees, and then use those degrees to earn enough money to pay their college-loan debts. However, you do not want to graduate from college with the heavy burden of loans to repay. There are a myriad of programs to assist in tuition costs.

MERCHANT'S WORDS OF ADVICE:

WHILE IN HIGH SCHOOL TAKE HONORS CLASSES EARLY. THEN TAKE ADVANCE PLACEMENT CLASSES ,SO BY THE TIME YOU ARE A SENIOR YOU CAN TAKE COLLEGE CREDIT COURSES LIKE ENGLISH, MATH, FOREIGN LANGUAGE AND HISTORY. BY THE TIME YOU STEP FOOT ON A COLLEGE CAMPUS YOU ARE ALREADY A SEMESTER OR YEAR AHEAD.

The amount of assistance you receive may be a critical factor in determining what institution you attend. Carefully consider those universities that offer partial/full tuition for high performance academically, athletically or otherwise. Don't make a decision as big as this out of emotion; be realistic and smart. Lay out all options.

There are plenty of different types of scholarships available — not just athletic and academic. I provide services on my website, http://www.thisiswhydoc.com, to assist in finding scholarships. But, there are many out there. A great point of reference is Joi Wade's book, "You Got Into Where? How I Received Admission and Scholarships to the Nation's Top Universities" and Starr Essence's book "Guide me to College: 10 Vital steps every urban youth need for college." The internet is your best friend when seeking scholarship money. Search online for opportunities. No scholarship is too small; a few hundred dollars here and there can add up very quickly. Apply yourself in high school academics and in your extracurricular activities to put yourself in the best position to be successful. Visit https://www.fastweb.com/ where you can create a profile to search scholarships and grants that fit your needs. Another website, https://www.scholarships.com, is a great resource to find all sorts of funding. Download the apps grants.gov and Scholly. I challenge you to go to these sites and spend an hour a day applying for scholarships. At the end of this section, you will see other links for related articles and websites for various scholarship opportunities.

Because of my grades in high school, I received a partial financial scholarship for college. I applied for and received additional, smaller scholarships as well. I received a half scholarship for Temple University and a full scholarship to Lincoln University – both in Pennsylvania. I had several scholarships that would have allowed me to attend different schools, but Hampton University was my top choice for my goals. One thing you must always keep in mind is that for many scholarships, there are requirements for either your education or your work after you graduate. This is especially true for scholarships that pay full tuition and board (e.g., housing/meals). For example, they may require a certain GPA or participation in a certain sports team or club.

Guidance counselors, mentors, and leaders in your community are great resources to obtain information about scholarships and getting as much free aid as possible.

Free Application for Federal Student Aid (FAFSA)

To receive federal and state aid, you must submit the Free Application for Federal Student Aid (FAFSA). Many colleges and universities, especially public institutions, also require the FAFSA. You must submit the FAFSA every year that you want aid. You award determination is typically based on your parent's income. It must be done in advance and yearly online or on your mobile device. Visit http://www.fafsa.ed.gov or call 1-800-4-FED-AID for more information.

The Faithful Few is another organization that assists with FAFSA and other resources for college. Its goal is "to leverage community support from our village members: parents, academic professionals, faith-based organizations and business leaders to offer the best opportunities. And through the support of all stakeholders, we will be able to support our youth in their journey to gain higher education and secure their future." You can find them at<u>http://www.thefaithfulfew.org</u>.

A great article describing the process for those individuals who are independent of their parents and have to fill out a FAFSA can be found at<u>https://www.fastweb.com/financial-aid/articles/how-do-i-become-independent-on-the-fafsa-if-i-am-under-age-24</u>.

Below are various scholarships I have come across from my own experience or through my network. Take notes, do your research, and learn from us.

Essays

Essays are important when filling out your applications for college and your applications for scholarships. Some require specific essays depending on the topic or the particular school. I would advise to you save every essay you write because you may be able to reuse the same essay and only have to change a few words around specific to what is required.

Joi Wade is a college student who wrote a book about her college application process and the journey she went through in making the decision. In Chapter 7 of her book "You got into where" She gives 10 tips about Essays for a college application. The same tips can apply to scholarship applications as well. Her tips are:

1. Start Early-Don't wait until the last minute

2. Think small-focus on the major points of the topic don't generalize multiple things

3. Avoid cliches and common topics-Be unique in your topic choice

4. Outline three different essays-give yourself options

5. Write your rough draft-tell a story in your essays and make conversational

6. Show your draft to at least three people for feedback-it's always good to show your network what you have and get constructive criticism

7. Rewrite and edit your draft-check for errors have others look it over as well

8. Rewrite and edit some more — make sure you create the best product you can

9. Take a break-take a few before you submit and look at it again with fresh eyes

10. Polish your final copy and print it to show it to one more person before sending it off

These are some great tips Joi came up with. I summarized them for you to have an idea from a current student perspective. I suggest reading her book as well.

Taylor Gribble, a student at Central Michigan University, was a summer intern with my company. She developed some essay questions to help you prepare for the essay portion on college and scholarship applications. Here they are below: (They are also list at the end of the book with space for notes)

SCHOLARSHIP ESSAY PRACTICE

Directions: Below are five sample essay writing prompts. In the space below respond to the sample prompts in detail. Be sure to use appropriate grammar and punctuation.

1. What do you expect to gain from earning a college degree?

2. Write a short essay that describes areas in your life where you showed leadership and overcame an obstacle.

3. Where do you see yourself in 10 years?

4. How would you handle the current issue of gun control?

5. How do you define success?

Scholarships and Grants

Scholarships and Grants are a great way to have college paid for. Nothing will fall in your lap. You have to go out and research. You will be surprised what is out there and how you can have college paid for just by doing what you are already doing in high school. Below are a few people who received various types of scholarships.

Band scholarships

Dominique Natasha Wilkins (http://www.shechicago.org/) is a proud Detroit Native currently residing in the great city of Chicago. After graduating from Cass Technical High School, one of the most prominent high schools in Detroit, she attended college on a full Presidential Scholarship and obtained a Bachelor of Science in Music Engineering Technology. During her college tenure, she became the First Female Head Drum Major in her University's history, sat 1st chair in the Symphonic Wind Ensemble and HBCU Band Consortium, and was initiated into Alpha Kappa Alpha Sorority, Incorporated.

"Being a diligent musician unlocked many doors, including academic ones, for me as a student. Because I worked really hard at my craft, I was able to audition for Mr. Barney Smart (former Director of Bands) and in addition to a band scholarship, he secured a Full Presidential Scholarship for me as well."

Gavin Mceachin is a college graduate from Long Island, NY. He went to high school and college with me and received a scholarship for band. Here is what he had to say:

"... I was undecided as to what my major should be. I took part in the pre-college program as I wanted to go out of New York State for school and be around students who looked and talked like me. I went to grade school in a predominately white school district in Half Hollow Hills, NY and I wanted to get the "Black

College Experience." I was told great things about college from James Yancy Merchant, who I grew up with in the same district. He was a year ahead of me. In high school, I played all sports and played saxophone in the school band. While at pre-college, I was drawn to the southern lifestyle and the soul of the Marching Band "The Force" when I saw them perform on campus. I saw a flyer on campus for open auditions and figured I would give it a shot. I knew I wanted to get involved with extracurricular activities. I landed a spot in the saxophone section while maintaining my decided major of Biology. After my sophomore year, I had come into my own in campus and through proven ability and social status, I was recommended for Drum Major for the Marching Band. Once I landed the job of Drum Major and finished my Junior year, I was offered a partial scholarship to stay on board The Force to help with my student loans. I was only offered a partial as I didn't major in Music, but since I carried at least one musical credit per year, I was qualified to be a recipient. So in looking back at things, if I hadn't taken advantage of the opportunities in front of me I wouldn't have been able to reap the benefits of being myself and doing what I loved to do while getting a great education."

Below is a link to a site that gives scholarship information specifically for music, but the website also provides information on over $2.7 million scholarships and grants. The money is out there. You have to do your due diligence to find it.
https://www.scholarships.com/financial-aid/college-scholarships/scholarships-by-major/music-scholarships/

Sports Scholarships

According to scholarshipstats.com, there are over 100,000 sports scholarships available for both men and women. That represents 34% of the total student athletes in college; a third of students who play sports in college are on scholarship. Their education is at least partially paid for by playing a sport. Now, imagine if you apply yourself in both the classroom and in sports in high school. That combination will give you a greater chance to choose the school you want and get a free education.

Here are just a few examples of some individuals who used sports to pay for their education:

- Dr. Timothy Frazier from Baltimore, Maryland utilized his talents as a high school quarterback to land a full scholarship to completely pay for his undergraduate education as a Biology Pre-Med major. That initial scholarship set him up to continue his education to become a medical doctor specializing in surgical orthopedics.

- Kellie Wells-Brinkley (http://kelliewellsbrinkley.com) 2012 Olympic Bronze Medalist from Richmond, Virginia was a Sports Management major and received a full scholarship for track and field due to her hard work and dedication to her talents in high school. Coaches visited her at high school and heavily recruited her to be a part of their program.

- Devin Green, a professional basketball player and Hampton University alumni, established his love for basketball at an early age. Originally from Akron, Ohio, Green received many basketball scholarship offers from many Division I mid- and high-major schools. Ultimately, Devin landed at Hampton University, where he played with the Men's Basketball Team from 2001-2005. Here are his words of advice:

"As I look back in hindsight on my career, the biggest advice I could share not only to the rising student athlete but also anybody in life would be to create a solid plan. You have to ask yourself, what does my life look like in the long term? If your goal is to play collegiate sports, the most important mindset is to have an overall vision of some college programs that interest you. This is a decision that will help shape the rest of your life, respectively. It's okay to take the time to be selfish for once. For the aspiring student athlete, study coaches and systems that the coach has implemented, then decide on a system that would put you in the greatest space for future success.

As I was in the process of choosing a University to attend, I reviewed everything I could in order to make the best possible choice for myself. I personally had trash bags full of offers from hundreds of Universities that ranged from high major to low major schools. With the combination of consulting with close family members and coaches, I ultimately picked Hampton University because it was the best fit for me as an individual.

Prior to your enrollment as a student athlete in college, be sure to understand that what you do in the classroom converts over to your sport. Doing well in the classroom usually leads to successful performance in collegiate sports. Take the time to take advantage of the resources that are available to you to prepare for your success on campus. Consult with your academic advisors and network with individuals that work very hard to make your time as a student athlete seamless. After high school, you must understand that the minute you step onto a college campus, you're currently in the business of sports, the faster you internalize that, the faster you understand how to be most efficient with your studies and most effective within your perspective sport.

Being a student athlete on the collegiate level is an amazing experience without question. You get the opportunity to represent your family, new peers (who most likely will become lifelong friends). Most importantly, you will have a connection to your college as your alma mater. When much is given, much is expected. This by no means will be an easy task. You will shed blood, sweat, and tears during your collegiate tenure as an athlete. In the end, you will learn many life lessons, and your experience will build you up to do great things. Good luck, and many blessings to all who have taken the time out to read this book. You're already ahead of the curve."

For more information on those available sport scholarships visit http://www.scholarshipstats.com/totalscholarships.html

Academic scholarships

Those 10,000 hours can be applied to classroom knowledge as well. If you have the skill of learning in the classroom and the talent to be a great test taker, you can use that to your advantage. If you have passion to learn, look at different professions and majors you are interested in. There will be colleges and Universities that will pay your tuition to attend just so they can say you graduated from there when you become successful. Here are just a handful of college graduates from my network who received academic scholarships.

Carrington Carter, a Chemistry Major scholarship recipient from Dayton Ohio said:

"Due to my hard work, discipline in high school, graduating with a high GPA, participating in extracurricular activities, and doing well on my SAT/ACT, I received a full academic scholarship to attend college. If you're in middle school or high school, there is absolutely a financial benefit to doing well in school. I would not have been able to build wealth to the extent that I have if I had student loans to repay from undergrad or grad school. I also received full and partial scholarships to several other schools, but what led me to choose Hampton University was a desire for the HBCU experience. My K-12 education was in a predominantly white (98%) school district, so I was looking for something different. I can honestly say that in many ways Hampton University is responsible for the life I enjoy today. My wife went to Hampton, my main business partner went to Hampton and it was at Hampton that I was introduced to the concept of building wealth and having your money work for you after reading the

national bestselling book Rich Dad Poor Dad in a freshman honors course. I grew up in a middle class household (both my parents also went to Hampton). However, in my house, just like many households, money was not frequently discussed. I learned the importance of saving and putting money in the bank, but that's essentially where my money education ended."

Ian Brown, a computer science major scholarship recipient from Sacramento, California said:

"I graduated HS with a 3.4 GPA, but like most other African-American kids, I would require financial assistance to go to college. To reduce the amount of money I would have to borrow and eventually pay back, my parents pushed the scholarship route. I applied for at least 30 scholarships locally and qualified for several partial scholarships offered by different HBCUs based on my high school GPA. I was awarded a partial scholarship and supplemented my first year and half with the local scholarship funds."

MERCHANT'S WORDS OF ADVICE:

"you miss 100% of the shots you don't take"

Apply for as many scholarships and grants as you can and as early as you can. Use the internet look up ways to have your college education paid for. Invest in yourself daily. You have a number of combined scholarships as well. You can have combinations of scholarships like a half academic scholarship combined with a half sports scholarship. Do your research. You never know if you don't ask and try. During my THIS IS WHY DOCUMENTARY interviews, an interviewee gave some of the best advice that I heard for a high school student so I'm going to give it to you. "Starting today, devote one hour a day researching scholarships and grants for college." Thats my challenge to you all.

Below is a list of suggested links for scholarships. Apply for as much as possible.

Download these apps grants.gov and Scholly

Www.fastweb.com -

Create an account and search various scholarships and grant offers.

https://www.scholarships.com -

A great source to find all sorts of scholarships. Go to this site spend an hour a day applying for scholarships starting at least your junior year in college

https://www.scholarships.com/financial-aid/college-scholarships/scholarships-by-major/music-scholarships/ —

Scholarships specific to music

https://www.usnews.com/education/blogs/the-scholarship-coach/2011/07/28/6-college-scholarships-that-award-leadership —

6 scholarships that award leadership

https://www.wxyz.com/news/Detroit-high-school-senior-is-accepted-to-41-colleges-awarded-over-300-000-in-scholarships —

Article on a high school student who was awarded $300,000 in scholarships and accepted to 41 schools

https://hbcudigest.com/uvi-becomes-first-four-year-hbcu-to-offer-free-tuition/ —

HBCU that offers free tuition

www.thehbcuhub.org/scholarship —

THE HBCUHUB scholarship program

https://www.tmcf.org/our-programs/career-preparation/apple-tmcf-hbcu-initiative

The Thurgood Marshall College Fund (TMCF) in partnership with Apple is proud to present the Apple HBCU Scholars Program

https://linktr.ee/emerging100atl

@emerging100atl emerging leaders scholarship

https://www.cleveland.com/news/2019/03/say-yes-to-education-students-at-Cleveland-state-university-will-receive-2-years-of-free-housing.html?utm_source=facebook&utm_medium=social&utm_campaign=clevelanddotcom_sf

Article on free housing for two years at Cleveland State University

https://money.cnn.com/2017/05/11/pf/college/Tennessee-free-community-college/index.html

Tennessee free community college for adults

http://www.fox26houston.com/news/isiah-factor-uncensored/university-of-Houston-downtown-offers-free-tuition-to-low-income-freshmen

University of Houston downtown offers free tuition for low income freshmen

Www.thefaithfulfew.org

"Our goal is to leverage community support from our village members: parents, academic professionals, faith-based organizations and business leaders to offer the best opportunities. And through the support of all stakeholders, we will be able to support our youth in their journey to gain higher education and secure their future."

https://howtosavemoneyforcollege.com/6095-grants-for-college

REFERENCES:

Joi Wade's *"You Got Into Where? How I Received Admission and Scholarships to the Nation's Top Universities"*

Starr Essence's book "Guide me to College: 10 Vital steps every urban youth need for college."

Take home messages

Merchant's New Face Method for success in college starts here on the High School Level

"Put your skills to work"

Remember 10,000 hours break and down and dedicate yourself

Get college paid for before you graduate

Know your plan: write it down. The goal is to have college paid for before you graduate

Apply for as many scholarships and grants as possible. Look for scholarships that fit your profile along with those that DON'T

Fill out your FAFSA with your parent or guardian (Done annually)

"you miss 100% of the shots you don't take"

THE DECISION THAT WILL CHANGE YOUR LIFE

Inspirational Person Day'nah Cooper-Evans

Know Yourself

What do you want?

Make a Decision: What school fits your plan?

Stay Local or Go Far

HBCU

Community college

Public vs private

Senior Guide

TIPS

Choosing a major

Personal Stories

Suggested viewing/reading

Takeaways

Know Yourself Assessment

INSPIRATIONAL PERSON
Day'nah Cooper-Evans

Day'nah Cooper-Evans is a recording artist, songwriter, vocal producer, and former professional dancer. She obtained her Bachelor of Arts degree from Hampton University in 2008. She won an NAACP Image Award in 2018 for her vocal production work on The New Edition Story on BET. Day'nah has performed as a background vocalist with artists including Fergie and Queen Latifah. She also works as a vocal producer for Queen Latifah for her personal music projects, as well as for the FOX hit television show Star.

Day'nah has worked in the studio with other acts including Mary J. Blige, Brandy, Janelle Monae and MagicA. N. T. and has written and produced tour content for Janet Jackson. She will also be featured as a singer on Netflix's upcoming sitcom Family Reunion. In addition to her career as a vocalist, Day'nah has also had a successful career as a professional dancer. She was featured as a dancer at Super Bowl 51 alongside Lady Gaga in 2017. She has also danced for and toured with artists including: Justin Bieber, Nicki Minaj, Diddy, Miley Cyrus, Snoop Dogg, and Christina Aguilera. Day'nah was also a cast dancer on the hit Disney television shows Shake It Up, A. N. T. Farm, and Kickin' It, as well as Nick Jr.'s The Fresh Beat Band.

Day'nah also has several entrepreneurial endeavors that she is working on including Caviar Cool, a music production company she runs with her husband, and a food truck business she co owns called Music and Mood which presents a gourmet Caribbean fusion menu while shedding a spotlight on up and coming artists in the music industry.

www.iamdaynah.com

iamdaynah@gmail.com

@IAMDAYNAH

-Dr. Shaundau Woodly in MC Mean Move The Class states:

"Our paradigms represent our perspective and it is from our perspective that we make decisions."

Know Yourself:

3 questions you need to answer

Who are you?

What motivates you?

What do you want?

When students start thinking about choosing colleges, they often get excited and want to jump right in. They think about location, party-life, and fraternities. At the end of this section, I recommend completing the brief self-assessment. This decision will be the most important one for the next four to six years of your life. This decision will set up your life moving forward. My method for success involves considering how happy and comfortable you will be in your new college environment. "The Decision" is imperative. Take it seriously.

No matter how old you are, no one knows you better than you know yourself. You spend 100% of your life 24 hours a day, seven days a week working on yourself. You may not realize it, but now is the time to think about what you want and how you can achieve it. Write it down, visualize it, and own it. There are some questions at the end of this section to help you.

Stephen Curry, two-time league MVP, three-time NBA champion when asked what he would tell the 2009 Stephen Curry in an article on www.undefeated.com by David Dennis Jr, he responded by saying:

"Find out who you are quick, because that's the foundation and the thing that you rely on no matter if things are going your way or not, if you reach your goals or not. Find out who you are, be comfortable with it, embrace it, and let that be the most consistent thing that you can rely on."

The quote above from Stephen Curry says it perfectly. When I talk to a teenager, I tell them to think about who they are right now. Find out who you are and accept the journey it has taken you to get here. Build off that and become the best person you can be.

Think about yourself and what you want in life. You've probably had some goals even at a young age. You've probably have plans even if they have changed over time. What charges you up? What gets you to be productive in life? Only you know what motivates you. Think about what you care about on a daily basis. Think about what wakes you up every morning. That is your passion and your drive. Stick to that and let that be the fuel for your success in life.

There may be someone reading this who isn't a potential college student. Some of you may be reading this to benefit someone else. If that is you, you are a motivator. As a motivator, you have a major influence on young adults. Use your passion to talk to young people about attending a college or University. And you can talk to them about the importance of answering some critical questions about their goals and motivation. For those motivators reading this, whether you are a parent, a mentor, a teacher, or simply a caring friend, give your young person an opportunity to self-access. Give your advice, yes. But don't force decisions on them. Support their ideas and encourage their questions.

Knowing yourself is important when deciding what college to attend. Influencers/motivators are great as guides who help with decision-making. However, parents and mentors sometimes make decisions based on their own insecurities and fears along with their own knowledge or lack of knowledge. Although parents feel they know what is best, ultimately the college choice should be the decision of the person who is actually embarking on this journey.

Listen to the advice I am giving you. Listen to the advice and stories of others in this book, and learn from us. I am writing this book after years of success. But it's the failures that have led to the most valuable lessons. Learn from both so that you can do better moving forward. I want you to be a thousand times more successful than anyone I have ever come across in my own journey. All the others associated with the production of this book feel the same way.

At some point, you have to figure out what you want in life. What are your goals? How you do you want to be successful. What do you want to be known you for? What do you want your legacy to be? Now, some people don't know what they want at age seventeen. It may be easier to just think about abstract ideas at first, or to consider what you don't want for your future. Maybe you have an idea of what makes you happy. Once you decide to do things that make you happy, no matter what it is, it's like you can work without feeling like you're working. There's an old saying. "Do what you love and you will never work a day in your life." So, what do you love?

Carl Grey is an entrepreneur from Maryland. He gives the following sound advice for anyone thinking about college.

"The BIGGEST piece of advice is PUT GOD FIRST! The 2nd biggest piece of advice I could give is: "KNOW WHO YOU ARE BEFORE YOU GO TO COLLEGE" I know that many say you go

to college to "Find yourself." HOWEVER, if you've been alive for 18 years, you should know who you are. The time that your parents spent raising wasn't for naught. The things that you did growing up that helped make you who you are, are not to be forgotten. Be open to change, new ideas, and methodology. But remember that YOU ARE NOT A BLANK SLATE. The "Blank Slate" mentality is one that attempts to get you to conform to how people with their own agendas want you to be. Not saying that there is any negative intent: however, it's important that you know who you are before you set foot on any campus. You want these new experiences to help you be more you. THAT'S how you make it."

Danna Purnell from Long Island, NY is a graduate of Suny Old Westbury with a criminology major. She started her college career at Mansfield University in Pennsylvania. Although she was on a full scholarship to play basketball, her decision to go to Mansfield was not hers. Therefore, she returned home.

"I did not have a voice. My father made the decision for me to go to that University. I had offers to play basketball since I was 11 years old, Seton Hall, Villanova, Wagner just to name a few — all full offers for Division I basketball and he chose for me to go to a smaller D2 school. Had it been my decision I would have chosen differently."

I know that I am talking about quite an early start to this process. If you happen to start later than I recommend in preparing for college, don't give up! It's never too late to save, research, and prepare for college for yourself or the youth that you motivate and support. Regardless of the timing, seek advice, develop a plan, and create a path for a successful college experience.

Making a Decision: What School Fits Your Plan?

The decision to go to college is a very big step for a 17 or 18 year old in high school regardless of whether they have scholarships, a patchwork of financial aid, or if they are going to have to figure some things out. No matter the background, the actual decision is very important and it should be made by the person who will be attending the College/University. Always take advice and do your research to gather information, but ultimately the final decision should belong to the person who is actually embarking on that journey. During my interviews with my peers for the THIS IS WHY documentary, I learned that some people ended up going to their college because they were told to. They didn't feel that they had a choice. Having the feeling that you can control your own future is very powerful and makes every experience that much better. Put serious thought into your decision to not only go to college but where you plan to go and why.

The minute I walked on to the Hampton University campus, I felt at home. The campus was beautiful and bright. It's called "your home by the sea" and it's easy to see why when you arrive. The landscape is teeming with trees. The people are friendly. It's a small family campus — very intimate for a college setting. It gives you a private feel being in the Hampton Roads area. The University is not in the middle of a city like Temple or Howard University. I knew that a quieter campus with a smaller student body would accentuate my own strengths and goals. Some people will fare better at a college in a city or with larger campuses and more students. Consider the kind of settings that have worked well for you in the past. Determine whether you need a change from what you are used to or if you want to be somewhere that fits in your comfort zone.

When I visited, I visited on my own with my best friend Sean Washington, rather than with a college tour. The campus was almost empty. I met some students at admissions and loved the visit. My cousin, Laquan Stewart, was the only family member I know who was in college at the time. He had attended Hampton University and was taking an extra year to complete his aviation degree, so he would still be there my freshman year. Laquan was my older cousin but not a distant cousin. I knew him. We were 5 years apart and had grown up together. We both were raised in Queens and until he left for Hampton, I saw him all the time. To have someone in Hampton, Virginia that's actually family, made the transition that much easier for me.

At Hampton, I didn't feel like I would just be a number on campus. I mean, Hampton was bigger than Lincoln University but not as big as campuses you see in movies.

To me, in movies, college seemed huge with these large lecture halls and everyone seemed like just a student identification number rather than like a real person. That's what I assumed college was going to be like until I visited Hampton's campus and found out the classes only had less than 25 students. Everybody seemed to know everybody by name. For me, that made a big difference. With the combination of my cousin still being a student, my best friend coming and the weather, I fell in love. Hampton was my choice moving forward. I was lucky to receive a partial scholarship, as well.

As I stated earlier, scholarships are actually an important part of how you make your choice for which college to attend. As I stated earlier, I actually had a few scholarships. Lincoln University gave me a full scholarship meaning my whole education would have been paid for. St. John's University gave me a half scholarship, which means I would have been able to attend for half the tuition price. I had others, I decided that Hampton was the best fit for me anyway, even though I didn't have a full scholarship.

MERCHANT'S WORDS OF ADVICE:

College is where you design your future. College will be your home away from home for not only the next 4+ years of your life, but will also impact where you go after that. You will start to build connections, experiences, and ideas for your future. Make college your home. You want to be around as much positive energy to enjoy every moment. I strongly suggest even if you decide to stay close to home for college to at least move on campus your freshman year and live in a dorm. You may think initially that having your own apartment off campus or staying at home is better but the things that take place and the independence you gain by living in a dorm your freshman year will help with your growth tremendously.

Stay local or go far

Part of your self-evaluation includes thinking about if you want to stay close to home or leave. It's a big decision. Do you want to stay in the same state or go across the country? Think about why you are answering the way you are answering. Does it make sense? Going to college close or far is a big decision and there should be multiple reasons why you are making that decision. Circumstances change all the time so you don't want to leave the decision a big as where you go to college to just one reason.

I am an advocate for leaving home to go to college because I strongly believe that people owe it to themselves to experience new people, places, and ideas. It's one of the ways you can make the most of your college opportunity. But that doesn't mean you HAVE to leave the state you live in. However, for me, leaving home and living on campus was a must! I had a half scholarship for St. John's University. I could have stayed in New York and went to school in Queens. Being that close to home for college wasn't what I wanted to do. I needed to get out and see what else was out there, besides New York. I wanted to see other places and meet people from other areas. I wanted to be able to feel and actually BE independent and not have to be under my parent's house. I knew it was best for me to leave the state.

Sometimes, the reason to leave a neighborhood is because you MUST leave to get away from negative things (e.g., gangs, toxic family, drugs, etc). This is very important to understand. If you are faced with negative or limited prospects for your future, leaving may be one of the best decisions you make in your life.

Have you heard of "out of sight, out of mind?" That means if you're gone, not only will you get away and forget about that lifestyle, the lifestyle will forget about you. And once you're gone, you will see how many other opportunities there are that don't include life behind bars. Not to mention there's a low chance you will meet a long-term romantic partner in jail. It's not CO-ED dorms there! Jail is never an option.

You, too, must get out of your comfort zone in some capacity. Sometimes that means leaving your home state in order to jump completely out of the nest. For others, just being an hour away or being far enough that going home takes a little extra effort is enough. The keys to successfully graduating outside the classroom still apply. Even if you live in Los Angeles and decided to go to UCLA 10 miles away from where you live, figure out plan to be on campus.

My strongest recommendation: DO NOT LIVE IN YOUR PARENTS HOUSE while in college.

Say goodbye. move out. Stay on campus for at least a year and then get your own place. Allow yourself to grow without relying on the support of your parents. Take the risk of the unknown. It's necessary to grow. It may feel uncomfortable but that's what will make you great and have your potential grow. There is no way to grow without making mistakes on your own and learning. Be thankful and grateful that there are people who have got you to this point in your life but now it is time to start to do it on your own.

Throughout this chapter are some personal stories of successful graduates and how they decided to attend college close to home or far away. These decisions shaped their lives and the lives of those they came across.

What Environment Are You Looking For?

Personally, I didn't know much about HBCUs in high school as I went to a primary white high school. Not many of my family members talked about college. But once I started asking around and actually visited an HBCU, I decided to attend one. I knew it was going to be my next home. I want to help create more awareness of the options for college especially going to an HBCU.

Historically Black College and University (HBCU)

HBCU is an acronym for Historically Black College and/or University. You will hear this term from time to time in this book and while you are embarking on the college journey.

HBCUs are a great opportunity for students who grew up in urban culture or for those who are the minority in high school and want a change. HBCUs will challenge your ideas about what it means to be a black student. You will meet people from all over the country regardless of whether you attend an HBCU, because college campuses are often diverse with many different cultures and nationalities learning together. However, at an HBCU, the majority of the student body will be African American.

Just to be clear, HBCUs exist because of segregation. The intention of HBCUs is not to segregate. Other races attend

HBCUs are welcome and accepted. At one point in our American history HBCUs was the only option for African Americans to attend college. As a proud alum of a HBCU, I can say that my college experience was made because of my decision to go to Hampton University and it would not have been the same any where else. This is why when you make a choice as to which type of University you want to attend be sure you understand and make the choice for you and no one else.

HBCUs traditionally are unique in many ways. For example, they are known for their bands and Homecoming events. This may be enough of a reason to persuade you to go to an HBCU. The bands are unsurpassed and, at homecoming, the feeling of being a part of a family is like none other at an HBCU. There are various people and organizations who are working diligently to increase awareness of HBCUs and the benefits of enrolling in one. You will see how the environment outside the classroom can have a major effect on your experience in college starting with the decision.

As an African American, going to an HBCU will allow you to go to college, learn your true history as an African American and realize that not every person that looks like you grew up like you and act like you. You will learn at an HBCU that the color of your skin does not determine your character and upbringing. There will be professors that are majority African American and faculty that you will be able to relate to on different levels. It's a great feeling to be the majority in not only a college setting but to have faculty, staff and peers that have the same goal of creating a better life for you and the next generation is something that is unmatched in a predominately white institution.

Edu, Inc.

Robert Mason is the founder of Edu, Inc., a black college application organization, where you can apply up to 53 of their listed HBCUs for only $35. The website is a great source of information. The company has a great track record. Thousands of students were able to get accepted to various colleges and received hundreds of thousands of dollars in scholarship money. https://commonblackcollegeapp.com/

HB1 network

Joseph Walters founded the HB1 network. It unites and celebrates the HBCU community on social media. Mr. Walters travels to various HBCU campuses, games, and events and promotes the greatness that is HBCUs. He also provides some historical background on HBCUs and specific colleges and universities on social media. Follow them on instagram @hb1network.

HBCU Connect

Ellen Dunn was an intern for my events planning company. She graduated from college and took the tools she learned outside the classroom and applied them as an educator. She started her own program in Maryland called HBCU Connect that aims to "promote college readiness, build community connections with HBCU students/alumni and visit schools." They also want to "heavily advocate for early acceptance and scholarship."

Set & Achieve Foundation, Inc.

Set & Achieve Foundation, Inc. is a Jacksonville FL based nonprofit organization that understands the importance of HBCUs. Founded by 5 HBCU alumni from various colleges, these peers congregated together to change the narrative that attending a Historically Black College or University is still dope! President, Chelsea Lewis worked at her alma mater Florida A&M University for five years in the School of Business & Industry and noticed a disparity in freshman enrollment. She began to ask high school students that she knew what college in Tallahassee would they be most interested in attending if they received a full ride? Almost every student selected FSU over FAMU. Challenged by this she joined her peers to develop a scholarship program that would funnel black dollars back into black schools. Thus, how the Foundation was formed.

Set & Achieve serves as a community resource guide for high school students and their parents, offering collegiate preparation assistance, professional development, mentoring, and grants scholarships to students that attend HBCUs. The Foundation hosts an annual HBCU Cookout which connects local alumni and in effort to promote HBCU unity throughout the city of Jacksonville.

For more information or if you would like to donate to this program you may do so by visiting: setandachievefoundation.org

Community College

A community college is a college that usually offers students a chance to stay close to home and earn vocational training, course credits to transfer to another college or university, and/or a two-year degree (e.g., associate's degree). Typically, a community college is less expensive than four-year colleges. For some students this is a great option to transition to college life more slowly, take core classes for less money and/or gain workforce training.

Jenar Harrison from Queens, New York graduated from high school and started his college basketball career in Junior college. He was then recruited and received a full basketball scholarship for American University, where he graduated with a degree in Communications.

My cousin, Tyrique Taylor, graduated from high school in Florida and moved back to Queens, NY. As his older cousin, I decided to take him under my wing and move him in with me in Virginia. I enrolled him in Thomas Nelson Community College in Hampton Roads. I wanted to give him an opportunity to see what else is out there. This gave him the experience of living in Virginia and afforded him the opportunity to go to a college that was affordable. It also forced him outside his comfort zone. Even though he eventually moved back to Queens, I believe that experience has helped him shape different goals in life and see the world in a different light.

Victor Rogers was an intern for my company, New Face Entertainment, Inc. Vic was originally from Texas. His family moved to Virginia and he attended Thomas Nelson Community College. When he completed his associate's degree, he was able to transfer most of his credits to Old Dominion University in

Norfolk, VA. He did his research and found out they had an internship program. He was able to use his college credits and his internship experience with my company, to graduate from ODU with his bachelor's degree with a major in marketing and a minor in management. He also became a brother of the Nu Theta Chapter of Alpha Phi Alpha Fraternity, Inc. and assisted the growth of the new student organization, Success without Limitations, becoming SWLs 2nd President.

Sometimes, people think of community college as a Plan B option when a four-year-college seems unlikely. However, you have to open your mind to community college as a good option to get away to better yourself. It's a good option for people who are considering how to NOT let money be a reason why you can't go to the university you want to go to.

Public vs Private

Tuition is probably one of the most important things to consider when thinking about public versus private institution. Public universities typically have state funding and so cost less to the student. Private colleges are mostly funded by the student and are much more expensive.

You have to pick a school you feel comfortable at a school that you can afford, and a school that allows you to grow. It's important that it be a school that YOU want, not a school that your family wants.

Go on college tours that give you variety. Look at the demographics of the school and ask about the various organizations on campus. See how many students are in the organizations you are interested in. If you want to join the football team, ask about the program. Be detailed in your questions based on what is important to you (e.g., how many players are on the team, what is the coaching staff like, how do they support student grades).

If you already know that you have aspirations to take part in Greek life (fraternities for men, sororities for the ladies), find out the number of members in the chapter and how active they are on campus. Also, most students don't know how much it costs to pledge or to live in a Greek house on campus. Ask about that! Investigate past lines (groups that have pledged a fraternity or sorority) and how many members are initiated into the campus chapters yearly. Check out some of the events they sponsor and look at their social media pages and hashtags. Follow them and see if you want to be part of their organization by seeing how active they are in the community and the type of events they host on campus.

When I went on my tours, I visited both private and public options. I saw Lincoln University and University of Richmond. Lincoln didn't seem like a good fit for me because I wanted to be closer to a city; Lincoln is in a country side in Pennsylvania. It was smaller than I was looking for. By comparison, University of Richmond was a large campus. I remember the basketball team towering over us in a cafeteria that reminded me of a mall food court. It looked great. However, the Black, male cheerleader who was showing us around seemed to have no interest in the job. He left us in his dorm room and went about his night. As I've said before, when I toured Hampton, I was home much different from University of Richmond.

You should identify your goals and consider costs, class size, culture, and environments before choosing your college. The experience will change depending on what you think is important and where you choose to go. Class sizes and demographics vary widely across school, too. Here are ten Universities to compare. All are Division 1 athletic schools, some are HBCUs both private and public.

Be advised the statistics are from 2019 and are subject to change every year.

Norfolk State (Public)

Norfolk, VA

5,000 students

2.9 HS GPA for incoming freshman

In State $6,000 $17,000 out of state tuition

The demographic is 86% in state and 14% out of state.

83% African American and 17% other

Hampton University (Private)

Hampton, VA

3,800 students

3.7 average HS GPA for incoming freshmen

Tuition $23,000

The demographic is 73% of state and 27% in state

95% African American and 5% other

The teacher to faculty ratio is 13:1

University of Notre Dame (Private)

Notre Dame, IN

8,500 students

$52,000 tuition

92% out of state 6% international 2% in state

68% Caucasian 10% Hispanic 22% other

10:1 student to faculty ratio

The Ohio State University (Public)

46,000 students

Columbus Ohio

In State tuition $10,700 out of state $30,700

Demographics

73% in state students 8% international students 19% out of state

68% Caucasian 5% African American 6% Asian 4% Hispanic 17% other

19:1 student to faculty ratio

Old Dominion University (Public)

Norfolk, VA

19,500 students

Average HS GPA for freshmen 3.29

$10,800 in state 29,772 out of state tuition

92% in state students 8% out of state students.

45% Caucasian 30% African American 9% Hispanic 5% Asian 10% other

18:1 faculty to student ratio

USC University of Southern California (Private)

Los Angeles, California

19,000 students

Average HS GPA for freshmen 3.76

$53,400 tuition

50% in state 35% out of state 15% international

40% Caucasian 20% Asian 14% Hispanic 5% African American 21% other

8:1 student to faculty ratio

Morehouse College (Private)

Atlanta, GA

2,202 students

$23,000 tuition

Private

All male

72% out of state

94% African American

12:1 student to faculty ratio

Mansfield University of Pennsylvania (Public)

Mansfield, PA

1,836 student population

$10,000 tuition approx. in state 18,000 out of state

Public

17% out of state 82% in state

10% African American 80% Caucasian

15:1 student to faculty ratio

University of Virginia (Public)

Charlottesville, VA

16,777 students

$13,000 tuition in state $44,200 out of state

4% international 28% out of state

6% African American 14% Asian 57% Caucasian

15:1 student faculty ratio

Hofstra (Private)

Hempstead, NY

6,800 students

Average HS GPA 3.6 incoming freshmen

$44,600 tuition

54% in state 6% international 38% out of state students

56% Caucasian 9% black 13% Hispanic 10% Asian 12% other

13:1 student to faculty ratio

*statistics from and for a list of more universities
www.petersons.com

For information on the Universities listed visit:

www.nsu.edu

www.hamptonu.edu

http://www.virginia.edu

www.hofstra.edu

https://www.mansfield.edu

www.odu.edu

www.usc.edu

www.morehouse.edu

www.nd.edu

www.osu.edu

Here is a monthly guide you should follow by your senior year in high school:

Apply for at least 7 scholarships and grants a week starting the summer of your senior year. (There is nothing wrong with starting sooner)

September

Register your ACT/SAT

Choose 5-15 colleges that fit what you are looking for

October

Take your notes and create a timeline of deadlines and requirements

November

Send in your transcripts and test scores

Complete your applications and finalized essays

December

Deadlines for scholarships should be coming up

April

Consider all your options and offer letters

Respond to the college you choose

May

Celebrate and prepare for High School graduation

Read THIS IS WHY YOU GO TO COLLEGE

Here are 4 tips on how to make the right choice. Each tip is directly related to knowing yourself and pushing your limits and the boundaries of your comfort zone.

1. Get Organized

Hopefully, if you are thinking of going to college, you already have some organization skills that you can use during this process. You must be organized in order to be successful not only in college but in life. I recommend that you keep what you learn about yourself, your college plans, and the information about colleges in some organized place. It will save you time when it is time to make your decisions. Because of the notes I took as I was going through this process, I was able to plan out things as perfect I can make them ahead of time.

You can contact me and my company directly for assistance in choosing the best college for you and any help needed in narrowing down your decision.

2. Learn

One phrase I live by is "every day, do better." This saying means that I do something every day that makes me feel like I'm growing or learning something. Living by this mantra can help you know that the day didn't go to waste. You have to get better somehow, in some way. Don't waste time; Don't waste a day. I've been learning and relearning that wisdom as I get older. In college, do not waste your time or anyone else's. Take time everyday doing better for yourself. A good trick is to take some time learning about people who have the kind of success (e.g., career, degree) that you are aspiring to. Something as simple as that will make you better! So learn about these colleges you are interested in and learn about the people that go there and that have graduated from there. YouTube the school get visuals , so on social media and use hashtags to find various details about the type of students that attend and what events they have. You can see for yourself and start to narrow your decision.

3. Stick to the plan as much as possible

It is critical to make a plan and stick to the plan as much as possible.

With that said, I am a firm believer in having multiple plan "As." You read that right. I don't mean that you should have a plan B, C, or D. Rather, you should craft a plan "A" and an alternate plan "A" that is equally as good as the first plan "A" For example, if you are bent on going to a particular University but you aren't accepted or you don't get enough financial aid, you need a second plan that was just as good as the first. This allows you to keep it pushing as if you there was no difference. That may mean having multiple options for college. When it comes to college, there are plenty of plan "A" options you can have.

4. Don't wait!

Here's a note for parents and other motivators: start the college process early, perhaps even as your child enters high school. There's also nothing wrong with looking at options, planning for campus visits, and exploring scholarships in the 8th and 9th grade. Expose your children to colleges and start installing the idea that education does not have to stop at the end of high school.

For my motivators of High School students: start as early as possible applying for colleges or at least looking at the application process. The students should have an idea of what one or two college campus looks like by the time you get to your junior year in high school, even if they saw them only on YouTube! The internet is a great tool to see what different colleges look like and have to offer before you actually get a chance to visit. By the time you get to 10th grade, you should have visited a couple of colleges and started developing an interest in the type of college you want to attend. During the 10th and 11th grade, you can start really considering locations and think about why you want to go to particular schools in particular states. Many parents don't realize how early you can start preparing for making a good college decision. It's also important to start thinking about college will be paid for. That is why it is smart to start early to plan and explore all options, like scholarships, which I will go into more detail in the next section.

Having a daily schedule is very important even while in high school. Here is an example by Taylor of how you may want to plan out your day. Insert the times you set aside for studying and the time of day you have the class. Structure like this will help you prepare for what they college routine will be like.

Monday	Tuesday	Wednesday	Thursday	Friday	Saturday	Sunday
Math						

English							
Science							
History							
Applying for Scholarships							

Choosing a major

Deciding what major to declare directly deals with knowing yourself and what you want in life. You may go into college, like myself, wanting to be a sports agent and then be told that a better plan is to study law and sports management classes. For me, I could not wrap my head around the idea of reading all those books to become a lawyer, especially when you think about going to law school after college. It was just too much for me to think about at 18-years-old. Instead, I put that time into starting my own event planning business. It seemed only natural to major in business management. Picking a major is an important decision but you can also change your mind. However, switching majors too often usually results in wasted time and money for classes that you no longer need.

For some people, it makes sense to start college without deciding on a major. It is acceptable to take general courses for the first year. This gives you time to look into all your options and figure out what field you want to pursue. Don't let a guidance counselor, or even a family member, tell you what major you should be. The decision needs to be 100% yours. Always ask advice, but don't let one person's opinion be the only one. Get a second and third opinion on choosing a major. And when you receive advice, listen for consistencies & inconsistencies.

Doing your research is important when choosing your major just like when choosing the university. Try to find out ahead of time how much schooling is needed in the field you are going into. Find out what additional training is needed after you graduate with your degree: do you need additional degrees (master's, doctorate, etc), licensing, certifications, or internships to be able to work in the field. You have to mentally prepare yourself for this journey. Knowing how much time you're going to dedicate in school is part of the battle. This is the beginning of your adult life. Mistakes will happen, the goal is to minimize those mistakes and align yourself to be the most successful person possible.

Jovan Brown, originally from New Jersey and now an educator in Brooklyn, NY, changed her major in the middle of college. She had this to say about choosing a major:

"Choose a major that edifies who you are; in this, everything you aim to pursue will find you because you've made room for it to."

"Selecting your college major can be a daunting or exciting experience. The latter is only achievable if you are intentionally thinking not about what you want to do, but who you intrinsically are. Because growth is destined to occur as you matriculate college, deciding on a major should be based in what you're truly passionate about-the thing that naturally brings joy to your stride and thoughts-the thing that gives rhythm to your life. I graduated from high school passionate about both English and Science. I

received excellence in both subjects, which made it quite difficult to arrive at selecting a major to once my season to be at Hampton rose upon me. I decided to enter as a Biology major, having convinced myself that I was going to leave Hampton to attend medical school to become a pediatric surgeon. But, writing and literature spoke to me in a way Science did not. At the onset of my junior year, I felt a tug to switch and therefore changed my major from Science to English. It caused me to graduate a year after the class I entered with, but it was the best decision I made. Choose a major that edifies who you are; in this, everything you aim to pursue will find you because you've made room for it to."

MERCHANT'S WORDS OF ADVICE:

LEARN A 2ND LANGUAGE EARLY. PICK A LANGUAGE AND STICK WITH IT THROUGHOUT HIGH SCHOOL AND IN COLLEGE. IF YOU DON'T HAVE A MINOR IN COLLEGE, CHOOSE A 2ND LANGUAGE AS A MINOR. TAKE A SEMESTER AND STUDY ABROAD. YOU WILL THANK ME LATER

Personal Stories: Going Far

Earlier I gave you some background on Dr. Howard Crumpton as an inspirational story. Had it not been for Dr. Crumpton's decision to go from Oakland, by way of Los Angeles, then to go to all the way to the East coast for college, we would have never met. This book and my company may have never existed as he was my business partner along with Sean Washington in forming Straight Face Entertainment. His cousin Phemi and my cousin Laquan were roommates, which led to our meeting. He made the decision to leave California because of his cousin who was in college at the time and his need for a change of environment.

Mya Brooks from Compton, California made the decision to go to Virginia. She knew she wanted to go to a Historically Black University (HBCU) but not specifically Hampton. Her first choice was Florida A&M (FAMU) prior to seeing the school, but after actually visiting multiple Universities she decided that Hampton University was the best fit for her. She actually has an identical twin sister who decided to go to Washington, DC for college at Howard University. Although identical twins, Makaila Brooks decided on another HBCU which is a much different college experience going to a University in a city like Washington, DC. All great choices but it really is incumbent on you to make the best decisions for you.

Josh Estrada is a college graduate also from Compton, California, made the decision to go to the East coast to play basketball. He wanted to get away from Compton and the city area. He wanted a University that gave him a feeling of having a home away from home. As crazy as it may seem, seeing students with mothers and fathers was something that drew him to Hampton University. Although Josh has both parents at home, coming from an inner city, He didn't see too many families with both parents. He notices at his freshman move in and tours that Hampton had students with strong family foundations and an overall home feel. Even though Josh chose a historically black college, he felt Hampton had diverse backgrounds and cultures that he wanted to expose himself to at a young adult age. One thing most people don't realize is that African Americans have different backgrounds and cultures. Josh at a young age recognized this early as he made his decision to leave home and explore something different from what he was used to.

Caron Washington brother to my best friend Sean Washington made the decision to go to East Carolina University in North Carolina. Coming from Long Island, New York he went to East Carolina on a partial baseball scholarship. He also enjoyed his visit and thought North Carolina was far enough from home where he was able to enjoy the independence and get the experience.

J'vonn Forbes is a Graduate of Morehouse University and an accounting major from Philadelphia, PA. He made the decision to go to Morehouse from being around male leadership growing up. He was told that Morehouse creates great leaders. He was exposed to leaders in the inner-city whether they went to Morehouse themselves or not. Those influences helped in his decision to not only go to an all-male college in Atlanta, Georgia but influenced him to stay. He eventually surrounded himself around people of similar positive minds and graduated.

Personal Stories: Staying Close to Home

Below are college graduates who made the decision to stay close to home but DID NOT live home. As I stated earlier, leaving home to go to college is essential to your growth and independence.

Nikki walker originally from Newport News, VA physiology major graduate of Hampton University and currently a teacher at Phoebus High School in the Hampton roads areaall schools within 20 miles of each other. She made the decision to stay local because the University felt like home for her and the decision was solidified because of family obligations.

Keion is from Hampton, Virginia business management major 2005 graduate of Hampton University decided to go to Hampton because of a local radio station 103 Jamz. He had no prior knowledge of college and was a military baby being that both parents were enlisted and traveled to different bases around the world. He heard about on site admissions for Hampton literally up the street from his home. He filled out the application after hearing a commercial on the radio station. Because of his high GPA and SAT scores in high school, he made the decision to go and sign up and was admitted right away.

Stan Wyatt was from Virginia Beach and was a Hampton University architecture major 2006 graduate. He actually wanted to go to another college, but the paperwork didn't go through in time. He wasn't pressed for college and felt like he couldn't afford it. But his family rallied around him providing him the support he needed to go. He always wanted to go to an HBCU, but Hampton was not his first choice. He didn't regret it once the decision was made.

Both of these men were enrolled in Hampton a year before me, and both are my great friends. Keion is my fraternity brother and someone I talk to constantly about life and plans to change the world. Stan actually was the original designer of my logo and printed shirts for my company.

Personal Stories: HBCUs

Bianca Cannon is from Long Island New York coming from the same high school always quiet and remained quiet throughout college. Bianca ironically was a cheerleader for the JV and Varsity team while I was on the varsity basketball team. During her interview of the THIS IS WHY documentary she stated that she didn't decide to go to Hampton because Sean Washington and I went there. She also didn't decide to go to Hampton Gavin Mceachin, Sean Gaddy and Costal Ernest went there. All who are our friends who we went to high school and college with. She went for her own reasons and found us there. Because of her experience and what she wanted in life. She learned about HBCUs through dance company, Venettes cultural workshop, her extracurricular activities outside the classroom in high school that persuaded her to not only go to an HBCU but Hampton University specifically. She also went on to Dance in college as well as a part of the Terpsichorean Dance Company along with a host of other organizations. She ended up going to Hampton but when she found out I am there along with fellow Hills west alumni, It instantly gave her the feeling of comfortability we all look for when your away from home. I personally feel like you need that in college.

Reginald Morris is from Northern Virginia and decided to go to college within a couple hours from his hometown. Here is take on going to a historically black college.

"First semester was hard, but only because I allowed it to be. Am I smart enough? Are my clothes good enough? Am I black enough to be at an HBCU? I had plenty of questions and not enough answers and it was driving me crazy. Growing up I was the perfect example of a big fish in a small pound. I was involved in everything, knew everyone, and generally thought I was the shit. My biggest mistake was not keeping that same energy. I allowed my circumstances to influence me as a person instead of allowing the person I know I am to reshape the circumstances around me. The best advice I could give to any incoming freshman is to RELAX. Everyone is awkward, nervous, and self-conscious; some are just better as masking it than others. You're going to be uncomfortable. You're going to be stretched in ways you've never imagined before. You're going to be pushed to the breaking point. It's OK keep going. Take risk, fail, learn, and overcome. Looking back you'll be grateful for the journey. Oh and by the way... you smart enough, questionable fashion choices are a part of the college process, and there is no such thing as "black enough" we're all Kings and Queens. "

We as a community have an obligation to give out as many options as possible when it comes to furthering our education.

Ellen Dunn is the founder of HBCU connect, an organization that helps teens realize their potential by promoting Historically Black colleges and Universities. She wrote:

"I believe the importance of HBCUs is so critically important, now more than any other time in history. During a modern technological and communication revolution meant to encourage "togetherness" and social awareness, minorities are still pushed to the margin.

We are still second class in spite of our many substantial contributions to society. As a high school student, I was aware of the many choices for higher education, but I ever only considered HBCUs. I admit I didn't care to struggle to be accepted at a PWI (predominantly white institution). Though I was young, I had already experienced my fair share of racially charged interactions with people not my skin color. Fast forward to now, I am an educator in a very diverse school, but my overall school system is still majority black. I am struck everyday with how beautiful it is to see young people learning, interacting, growing together regardless of their race. But, everyday I'm also irritated with how underrepresented we (blacks) still are, even as the majority! My school is a Career, Tech & STEM school, best is the county and top ranked in the state. We educate the best and brightest scholars and athletes, 70 percent of which are black. Because of this we have many at least 100 partnerships with institutions of higher education, however, HBCUs were sorely missing from Top tier talk.

I started the HBCU Connect Club, which was inspired by an already established organization meant to connect alumni and offer scholarships. Many of my students and sadly many white teachers and admin had no idea what an HBCU was. I strive to expose any interested student (not just African American) to ALL of their higher education options. I celebrate HBCUs and the rich history and accomplishments that these students don't know *about. We highlight a different school every week, take trips to local HBCUs, attend HBCU college fairs and invite HBCU alum to speak about their school/experiences. We also have an open discussion about current events that deal with education, HBCUs, PWIs and race relations in every facet of society. Last year was our first year and we held steady at about 15-20 students a meeting, this year we have grown to an average of 30 each meeting. I will be graduating four students, all of whom will be attending an HBCU in the fall!"*

The HBCU Hub, Inc. is a non-profit organization founded for the primary purpose of spreading HBCU awareness to students in the NYC tri state area (New York, New Jersey, Connecticut). The Hub also seeks to support recruitment to HBCUs and serve as an overall HBCU advocacy center. For more information visit http://thehbcuhub.org. The site offers scholarship information, access to various HBCU alumni, events in the area, and a full listing of HBCUs.

Jaaye Person-Lynn, Esq. attorney at law wrote this about leaving Home and creating a new life for yourself.

"Many remark on the bravery it took to move across country at 17 years old to go to a school I had never seen. Truth is— I left home to go home. My mother's parents were both Virginians: her father from Emporia and her mother from Windsor, just 25 miles from Hampton's campus. My grandmother was an only child, but my grandfather had almost 20 siblings, many of whom had children, and at the family reunion in 1997 in Virginia, based on the welcome I received from family, I was going to college in

Virginia, at an HBCU, with Prestige. Hampton was an easy choice. Despite the ease of that choice, the transition from Los Angeles to Hampton had challenges. The weather and culture I had never really experienced was rough early on. Still, in my first semester, despite the difficulties, like homesickness, December 10, 2000, was a harsh reminder I was in the right place. That night, my best friend was shot and other close friend killed riding in a car together down Crenshaw Boulevard. The seat Kevin was sitting in was a seat I had ridden in hundreds of times, down Crenshaw Boulevard.

The unfortunate news came while studying the night before my first collegiate final. My first winter break was spent at hospitals and Kevin's home going services. It was a real life reminder of how my physical environment affects my life. Over the next few years, I would hear story after story of people being arrested, being shot at, and all kinds of money-making schemes that usually ended badly. All the while, I was in my safe haven, Hampton University. Though there were real consequences for my actions at Hampton, the life and death stakes weren't as high as they were in the streets of Los Angeles and Inglewood. Maybe I make it to where I am if I went to a local college, but the physical departure from Southern California from ages 17-24 was the best decision I ever made. Navigating life as a young adult in the USA, especially a young male Descendant of American Slavery is difficult on many levels. From December 1998, when I started driving, until the summer of 2003, I had been pulled over twelve times by LAPD, LA Sheriffs and Inglewood PD. Three of those stops were legitimate, the other nine were wholly unnecessary.

This as the main inspiration for the abolitionist work I do now. In California, Black men make up 3.3% of the State's population and 27% of the prison population. Talking sheer numbers, that's an extra 30,000 Black men locked up, per capita. According to the Public Policy Institute of California, "The incarceration rate for African American men is 4,180 per 100,000. White men are imprisoned at a rate of 420 per 100,000, and imprisonment rates for Latino men and men of other races are 1,028 and 335, respectively." This is affirmative action and it taught me that, though California is known as the Liberal bastion of America, what California does more liberally than anyone is lock up Black men.

Hampton University, and subsequently Howard University School of Law, not only provided physical protection from the harsh world while I gained the tools needed to do this work, it gave me a community to belong to and Institutional Support beyond my family. It also made me part of a worldwide network of Social Engineers and all around dynamic people. The time spent on campus is the tip of the iceberg. Almost daily, my life is enhanced by a connection I made while in school. Feeling part of something greater than I, greater than my family, which provided the Foundation to my Foundation, is why I can never feel alone in this struggle, and why I can, as Dr. Harvey Charged all Hampton graduates with for the last 40 years, "Fight racism wherever it rears its ugly head."

Suggested Viewing

"We are rising" is a documentary where you learn about HBCUs and their rich history Available on Netflix

Sources of Information

https://theundefeated.com/features/future-hall-of-famer-Stephen-curry-whom-so-many-doubted-is-headed-home-for-all-star/

https://www.theodysseyonline.com/why-getting-away-from-where-you-grow-up-is-important?utm_source=Facebook&utm_medium=Owned+Social&utm_campaign=Aud+Dev

https://www.merriam-webster.com

https://diverseeducation.com/article/118831/

https://nces.ed.gov/fastfacts/display.asp?id=667

https://www.usnews.com/best-colleges/rankings/hbcu

Student loans webinar Joey Zachery https://www.makemoorcommerce.com/

https://theundefeated.com/features/how-did-north-carolina-at-become-the-countrys-leading-producer-of-black-engineers-care/

The Decision

TakeAways

Merchant's New Face Method for Success for High School Students

Make a plan and stay organized during the decision process

Take advice BUT choose a college for yourself

Do you want to "stay local or go far" why?

What type of college is for you? (community college, HBCU, Public, Private)

Your major should be your interest, your passion what you love

Know Yourself Assessment

"Your perception is your reality."

Even if you know these answers, I want you literally write them down. It's much different to see them organized on paper. Use extra paper if you need it.

What do you want to do after you graduate High School?
_____
_____
_____

What charges you up? What are you interested in every day?
_____
_____
_____

What makes you happy?
_____
_____
_____

What are your goals?
_____
_____
_____

What is your definition of success?

_____
_____
_____

How can going to college help you be successful and achieve your goals?

_____
_____
_____

What is your current network?

_____
_____
_____

Do you need your network to grow in order to achieve your goals?

_____
_____
_____

Do you want to go far or stay close to home? Why?

_____
_____
_____

STOP WHAT YOU ARE DOING!!!

Enjoying the read??

Take a picture holding the book, post it on social media

And hashtag #thisiswhyyougotocollege

BUILDING CHARACTER LEADERS NOT JUST SUCCESSFUL LEADERS

Inspirational Person Ashley Company

Inspirational Person Vic Rogers

Intangibles

Body language

Be an active listener

Effort

Being coachable

Motivation

Accountability

Having a sense of urgency

Ask Questions

21/90 rule

Chivalry and Respect

Network

Communication

Quotes

INSPIRATIONAL PERSON
Ashley Company

Inspired by a dream, Ashley N. Company made a bold move to leave her position as a District Manager with PepsiCo, a Fortune 100 company, to travel half the world's countries, learn new languages, and experience different cultures. Ashley, world travel expert and international speaker, is the social entrepreneur and visionary force behind **Jelani Women Travel and Jelani Girls, Inc.** Utilizing a dual-purpose structure, she curates cultural immersion and service trips for women of color traveling to Africa, while simultaneously raising funds to recreate the experience for underserved youth in South Africa and the United States.

As a global activist and speaker, she has started a movement for women and girls of color to reimagine Africa and redefine their concept of community and identity—a testament to the powerful results that are generated when passion and purpose are strategically aligned. With over 10 years of experience in youth development, mentoring, personal experience, and community organizing, Ashley N. Company has delivered transformational keynote speeches, workshops, and retreats to a wide array of audiences, designed to promote social engineering and self-discovery.

Ashley has been featured in multiple national and international media sources most notably CNBC Africa and Essence. She is an active member of Delta Sigma Theta Sorority, Inc. and the World

Affairs Council. Ashley has also been honored by the Foundation for Enhancing Communities with the 2014 Women In Philanthropy Award and Hampton University's Top 40 Under Forty Young Alumni Award.

Ashley N. Company

CEO & Speaker Jelani Girls, Inc.

New York:+1.877.282.4425

Johannesburg: +27.71.825.8475

AshleyC@jelanigirls.org

INSPIRATIONAL PERSON
Victor Rogers

Victor Rogers wants to ensure that his efforts make a difference and he has chosen to be part of the change that he wants to see in the world. Currently, he is serving as the President of the Urban League of Greater Richmond Young Professionals (ULGDYP). Victor joined the ULGRYP movement in September 2012 with a sincere desire to be involved and great ambition. In August 2013, he was appointed to serve on the National Urban League Young Professionals (YP) – National Programs and Awards Committee by the organization's Chairman, Travis Townsend. Victor comes to the YP movement with more than 10 years of civic activism that includes his journey with the National Association for the Advancement of Colored People (NAACP) branch in Hampton, Virginia but traces back to an inspirational influence — his grandmother, Ann Wagner. Mrs. Wagner is a lifetime member of the NAACP and 2010 Kentucky Commission on Human Rights Hall Of Fame recipient. Victor is the oldest of two children and a self-proclaimed "Army brat."

He graduated from Old Dominion University (ODU) where he earned a Bachelor of Science degree in Marketing with a minor in Management. During his time at ODU, Victor helped establish a student organization named Success Without Limitations, LLC (SWL). Upon Victor's graduation, he expanded the student organization to the campus of Virginia Commonwealth University (VCU) and the campus of Virginia Union University. With three locations, this grassroots, community driven, workforce development and job placement program is positioning itself in a manner that will help the organization achieve its primary goal to increase post-graduation employment rates among Virginia students. In June 2014, Victor graduated from the Emerging Nonprofit Leaders Program (ENLP) facilitated by VCU and the Partnership for Nonprofit Excellence. The ENLP is a dynamic eight-month experience for the next generation of nonprofit leaders in metro Richmond that focuses on strategic leadership, organizational change, collaboration, and coaching.

Victor uses his education and experience as a Full Life Cycle Recruiter at Astyra Corporation. Astyra Corporation is a minority owned computer and technology specialist staffing firm. Although he's a passionate community activist, Victor modestly acknowledges the variety of roles that he plays within the community. He is the Immediate Past President for the Xi Delta Lambda chapter of Alpha Phi Alpha, Immediate Past Chair of Alpha Day On The Hill, and current Eastern Region Director of College Brothers Affairs. Within the fraternity, he has also served as the political service arm for the national program, A Voteless People is a Hopeless People leading the VACAPAF (Virginia Chapter of Alpha Phi Alpha Fraternity) inaugural Alpha Day On The Hill. Additionally, he is an involved member of the board for Children Inc.; he sat on the Greater Richmond Chamber Community Affairs Committee for Workforce Development and Education; he is a former member of the Richmond branch of the NAACP; and a graduate of the City of Richmond's 18th Annual Citizens Police Academy.

These roles of support and leadership within the community have helped him build associations with like-minded citizens who are familiar with his desire to aid the Richmond community and bring continued positive change to the greater metro area. Just as his grandmother inspired him and was honored as a recipient of a prestigious award; Victor received the President's Volunteer Service Award – Gold (PVSA) during the year of 2014. The PVSA is the premier volunteer awards program, encouraging citizens to live a life of service through presidential gratitude and national recognition. The award is a tremendous honor and was presented on the national service holiday of Martin Luther King, Jr. Day, January 19, 2015. It is issued from the President of the United States of America and The White House and requires 500+ hours of volunteer service. Victor believes it is important to build strong relationships and commits time to his loved ones family and friends. He enjoys mentoring youth, preparing for competitive races, and cooking great tasting food. A fun fact: throughout his entire educational career — he attended 13 different schools.

I FELT THIS SECTION REQUIRED TWO HEADS AS OPPOSED TO ONE. SO, I ASKED THE FORMER VICE PRESIDENT OF NEW FACE ENTERTAINMENT, INC. AND COLLEGE GRADUATE, KARSON AUSTIN, TO CO-WRITE IT WITH ME.

Based on my method for success, the following terms will be important to learn. I took a few excerpts from my book **THIS IS WHY YOU GO TO COLLEGE: How to successfully**

graduate in REAL LIFE Studies Outside the classroom... and beyond. I want you to familiarize yourself with them and consider them while going through your daily routine in High School. IF YOU KEEP THESE INTANGIBLES IN MIND DAILY IT WILL PUT YOU FAR AHEAD OF THE COMPETITION. These are real terms and ideas for you to think about and practice every day. Thinking about these intangibles will open your eyes and put the things you do into a different perspective. As you begin to grow and utilize these skills, you will see a difference in yourself and others around you. Educators call some of these intangible skills you can learn and apply outside the classroom "soft skills" in comparison to subjects like math, science, and history, which you learn in the classroom. There is nothing soft about these skills. They are just as important, if not more important, because you apply them in your everyday life and in the work field. Being aware of and working on these intangibles will not only set you up for success but will build your character up to be a successful leader.

1. Body language

Body language is one characteristic you have full control over regardless of talent. Body language is defined as the process of communicating nonverbally through conscious or unconscious gestures and movements. Body language can speak volumes long before the first words are spoken in any situation. Poor body language can derail any interaction regardless of the value you are trying to present. Poor body language is one of my biggest pet peeves and should be yours as well. Facial expressions, posture, fidgetiness are all examples of body language. Whether I'm coaching a game, conducting a meeting, or helping to build a team, body language is the first thing I use to help get my point across. I use my stance, gestures, and eye contact. It can immediately change how a message is being perceived.

Let's say a woman is talking to five friends about a crazy night she had last night. She's excited to tell her best friends about this night that started off with going out with one of the greatest guys she ever met. But, one girlfriend is not engaged in the conversation; her eyes are not looking in the direction of the speaker. Two other girlfriends have their arms crossed with a "get to the point" look. The other two keep shrugging their shoulders like they could really care less about what she is talking about. How quickly would the woman's excitement dampen until she thinks, "Maybe my night wasn't as good as I thought it was?"

You could tell from the body language of these friends that they weren't really that into the story. Now, take that same example and all five friends are looking directly at the speaker hanging on her every word. Their body language is communicating that they are engaging as she relays every detail of her amazing night. It's the same story, but now she walks away thinking, "It was the best night of my life."

We have all been there before. We have all been victims of or witnessed poor body language. I want you to do a stellar job of being mindful of your own body language on a daily basis. If you see the body language of others is causing a negative result in a room, talk to that person in a positive way if it's appropriate to do so. I am quick to tell people to keep their heads up. I would suggest you smile at the person, ask what's wrong, invite them to stand to help ensure they are paying attention. Encourage them not to cross their arms when someone is speaking. How you present yourself affects how you communicate and how positive or negative your experiences will be.

Be mindful of your body language both when presenting information and when receiving it. Your body language must match what you are trying to convey. When your appearance conflicts with what you are saying, it can be confusing and can send mixed messages to your listener.

Body language includes your entire body. Your eye contact, facial expressions, arm placement, hand movements, stance, and posture are always speaking for you especially when you are not speaking aloud. Your body language can be interpreted from a distance, so be mindful of these things at all times.

2. Be an ACTIVE listener

This is not just actively waiting to talk. Make mental notes of key points you want to share when someone is speaking to you. That way, once you are given a chance to speak, you can respond to the most vital issues being discussed. When others are speaking, try to think about the exact words they are using. If you practice this, you will comprehend and retain a vast majority of the information you hear.

This seems like the easiest thing, right? Just listen. You have two ears and one mouth because God wants you to listen twice as hard to respond effectively. Use them. Listening is very important in any relationship, no matter the level. It is important to listen to your peers just as much as it's important to listen to your leaders and your mentees. If you take the time to listen to what people are saying without trying to a built-in response based on what you "know " they are going to say, you might be surprised to find that you are a terrible listener. Try this the next time you are at a workshop or having a simple one-on-one conversation. While you are listening, take notes about what they are saying. When they are done, repeat in your own words (this is called paraphrasing) what was said back to them and see how they think you did. You may think you are listening but did you hear the message? Do they think you missed any key points? Learning to listen takes a lot of time and maturity, but it's one of the best skills you can have. It will help you get through college, personal relationships, and life as a whole. You must hear and pay attention with thoughtful intent.

Try not to listen with intent to speak. Be sure to listen with the intention of gaining understanding of what the other party is relaying to you. This will help you develop follow up questions or may even answer the current questions you have. Understanding what is being said will be instrumental in preparing the next steps of what you are trying to accomplish.

Many underlying messages can be received by active listening. Sometimes things are not said clearly and directly, but if you listen, you can see the direction that the conversation or interaction is headed.

3. Effort

Some people say effort can't be taught. However, how many times have you heard "he's not even trying" or "she needs to at least try to do it." That's the power of effort. You want to try to utilize your day effectively in high school. You have the same 24 hours, seven days a week as everyone else in the world. That is the same 24 hours that your friends, enemies, celebrities, and billionaires have. You can put forth the same or more effort to achieve your goals in life by waking up with the intention to attack each day and make it better than the last. Effort is just your attempt to do something but I want you to look at effort as a gauge to determine how much you put into something. You can put in a little effort or a lot of effort. Let's say you are watching a basketball game. A team is getting blown out by 20 points. If the team gets discouraged and stops playing their best now, they could lose by 30. If the team gives the game an extra burst of effort and gives the game their all, they could make a comeback and end up winning by 10. This difference in result directly reflects differences in effort by the team. Put forth the effort to be successful. Effort and how much you care about what you're doing go hand and hand. If you genuinely care about what you are trying to accomplish, your effort should reflect that. Distinguish yourself from others in your field by always putting in "maximum effort." Don't ever lose the game of life because you decided not to give enough effort.

Care for and take pride in your work. That doesn't just apply to what you do in the classroom, it applies to all areas of your life. You should want whatever you're a part of to be a success and you should take it personally when it's not. It should hurt to the core that things didn't go the way initially planned. You should do everything you can to make it better moving forward.

4. Being coachable

Being "coachable" does not only apply to students who are on a sports team. This also applies to those who are a part of ANY team! Being willing to learn is very important. Even if you're the leader of a team, you still have to listen to the other members. You still have to be able to take criticism and interpret it in a positive way, even if it's presented to you in a negative way. If your coach is screaming at you to run a play a particular way, don't put your head down and tuck your tail between your legs. Take it as a motivation to get faster and stronger. Keep your head up and consider how to take in the recommendations to get better. And maintain a positive way of thinking.

5. Motivation

Motivation is your reason for doing something. Before you take on big projects, ask yourself what drives you to wake up every day and tackle your goals? Every day, I get up with the long-term goal of changing the world. My plan by the time I leave this earth is to leave my mark. That means that I want multiple people to have been positively affected by my actions. That is the number one reason why I wrote this series. I want to inspire people. I want people to read this and change their view on college. I want you to understand that college is not just about going to get the degree. Going to college is more than just sitting in the classroom and learning from a textbook or lecture. That goal is what motivates me right now. My long-term goal is to change the world and one way I am doing that is with the short-term goal of writing this book. I want to put it in the hands of millions of people! I have to get up every day and dedicate time to creating a successful publication for the world to read. What is your motivation? If you have not already done so, consider going back to the access yourself activity in section one. That can give you information about your motivation.

6. Accountability

You are responsible for your actions. Always hold yourself and your peers accountable as well. Accountability is important when you have set goals, especially when you are taking on a new challenge, like college. You no longer have an adult telling you to get up in the morning and go to high school. If you don't get up and take care of business by going to class or an organization meeting, it is 100% on you. It is a great idea to have friends and be accountable to each other. Create a network of like-minded students. It's called having an accountability partner or team. Accountability partners are commonly used for diets or workout plans. You can use accountability partners for anything. It's an easy way to ensure that you and your peers are successful. Some people utilize social media as an accountability partner. Make a post that everyone will see. It can help you feel like now you have no choice but to complete the task, especially if people ask you about it. For example, someone will post "I will lose fifteen pounds in two months." Then, they can post weekly updates on their weight loss journey. Their friends can follow their journey, make comments, give suggestions, and give encouragement. That is a way to use social media as an accountability partner. But first, be accountable for yourself. Really stop and think about what you need to do to be successful. No one knows you like you do. So if, for example, you know you need 30 minutes to get up and get out your apartment or dorm room, you have to be accountable to yourself to know that planning for that 30 minutes is essential. I give myself personal accountability goals all the time. I write them down everywhere. I repeat them to myself and others. I continuously talk about my goals in life and speak them into existence. The reason I do that is to make myself accountable because if I kept it to myself, I would be less likely to get it done.

Keep in mind when dealing with accountability that procrastination can occur. It happens to all of us. You hear or know you have to do something that you have weeks or months to complete. Before you know it, the time is up. Now you are rushing to complete the task and don't give your all because you don't have time. You must be productive everyday throughout your time, especially in college. There is so much "free time" in college, you may feel like there's nothing to do. However, one of the major learning experiences in college is figuring out how and when to do things on your own without any "adult" supervision because YOU are an adult now. If you are a part of an organization or get assigned with a task from your peers, no matter how long you think you have to get it done, do it as soon as possible. This extra time allows for any mistakes and ensures that the task is completed well.

7. Having a sense of Urgency

I deal with high school and college students on a consistent basis. I have noticed that the ones who treat tasks they set out to do like checking emails, ideas, plans, work as if it must be done by a certain time or day, they end up more successful overall. Having a relaxed attitude doesn't get things done and by the time it is done too much time has gone by where you could have missed out on other opportunities and/or learned much more. When you have a sense of urgency and avoid as many distractions as possible, that kind of focus on a daily basis will keep you ahead of the competition. That means doing tasks ahead of time. That means caring about your work. That means don't procrastinate.

8. Ask questions

I learned this in college and it has stuck with me to this day. Always ask questions. Ask three questions a day. When you are in class, in a seminar, or learning something new, ask questions. Even if you feel like you know everything... Ask questions. Asking a question can go so far and can lead to other ideas and goals. It also shows the people you are with that you are engaged and interested. We always can learn more. Everyone has been a teenager and I know at that age you think adults don't know everything. And it's true, adults don't know it all but neither do teenagers. So it's nothing wrong with asking questions and finding out information. Ask the same question to multiple people maybe that will make you more comfortable getting the correct information. Feed your brain with as much knowledge as possible.

9. 21/90 rule

I'm a firm believer in the idea that it takes 21 days to make a habit and 90 days to build a lifestyle. If you can commit to 21 days of working hard and actually trying to get better at something, you will be better than you were in the weeks prior. When you take it a step further, it takes 90 days to build a lifestyle. Consistency is the key, here. Three months of consistency and building a lifestyle change can go a long way in accomplishing your goals. You cannot continue to do the same thing over and over again while expecting a different result. The same applies while in college. You change your environment but you also have to change your habits.

10. Chivalry and respect

Just plain simple human decency can go a long way on a daily basis. Smile, say good morning and good afternoon when you see people walk past you. Men, open the door for women. Women, say thank you and smile. Of course, Ladies, you can open the door for us, men, too. We can also smile and say thank you! Remember the golden rule: Treat others the way you want to be treated yourself.

11. Network

I knew at a young age I wanted to be successful – whatever it was. I had been working since I was sixteen and played multiple sports. I rarely needed to be told to stay busy. I stayed engaged doing things I wanted to do with friends who had the same interests. Your network is very important as to which direction you will go in life. Your network, believe it or not, starts with your friends and extended family. They are your influencers outside of your home. Although you always need to have independent thinking to be a leader in life, it is paramount to build a network and lifelong friendships that support your goals. It may be on you to help shape your own friends into being successful leaders. Build each other up. That comes with the territory of being a leader. Motivate your network to be the best person they can be, and you will benefit each other.

You need to P. L. A. N. You need Proper Leadership to Access and create a strong Network. I know I was put on this Earth to create leaders. That's my purpose. To prepare your network you need to be a leader. A follower can't take full advantage of a network. That means you need to step up in a number of ways. That means being the strongest person in the room. That means taking advice and learning from those before you. That means being a positive influence on your peers and those coming after you. In high school that's taking initiative and doing what's right ensuring that you and your family and friends are headed in a positive direction.

I don't know everything, but I do know different people that are capable of getting things done. People contact me all the time about the most random issues: working out, schools, businesses, stocks. I am not an expert in any one field, but I do know someone in nearly any field that will know what you need. I've been able to help people with various issues from graduating from college, to getting community service hours, to buying a house, to investing. You name it, I've been able to help someone with it. I have been able to connect people in order for them to be successful in their endeavors. All because of the network I have built and the strong relationships I have kept with people.

Calling someone just to see how they are doing or supporting their ideas and businesses can go a very long way. Having an open ear to listen or give advice means a lot to anyone. Just being a genuinely good person goes a very long way. Being helpful and being a reliable person and a person of your word goes even farther.

Learning the art of networking and being able to utilize that network is very important even before college. In *Guide me to college by Starr Essence* there is a great list for high school students to start looking to build your network. Here are several that chose from that list and from my experience:

- Volunteering at events
- Starting business (teen entrepreneurs)
- Blogs and social media
- Summer youth jobs
- Community Service
- Religious youth ministries
- Peer leaders/counselors
- Fraternity/Sorority mentorship programs

12. Communication

I talk to my network of friends and business partners all the time about this. One of the biggest mistakes we make is assuming that everyone thinks the way we think. Communication is defined as "the act or process of using words, sounds, signs, or behaviors to express or exchange information or to express your ideas, thoughts, feelings, etc. to someone else." ~ Merriam-Webster Dictionary

The way you interact with people consistently or even on the first meeting can determine what kind of relationship you will have with that person moving forward. You have to be able to properly communicate. In today's society, you can communicate solely by email, text, phone, and social media; you could hardly ever actually see the person. These are all ways of communication that you have to use. I personally enjoy communicating in many different ways. At the same time, some situations call for certain forms of communication. Intention and tone of voice are often communicated differently by text or email and words can also get lost in translation without being able to see the person's nonverbal communication cues.

There are some consistencies in each form of communication. I will break them down to you.

- When you say you will do something, do it. No matter the form of communication, you are accountable for your actions. Your word is your bond. Everyone has a different sense of urgency, so if you are delegated a task or if you delegate a task to someone, be accountable and hold that person accountable to the schedule. Communicate ahead of time of the time or date given is often sufficient. Agree and hold each other to it. Things come up, we know, so just be sure to communicate any issues and plan for the adjustments. Anything can be accomplished with proper planning.

- Be consistent with how you communicate. If you're in a leadership position, you have to be a leader and communicate with respect. You should also expect respect back. Consistency also deals with being available. You have to be able to find time to communicate, even if the text is your primary form of communication. Be available daily by text. It doesn't have to be all day. If you are only available during certain hours, make those hours known. Communicate that. Be sure to leave communication lines open to those who may need to address problems with you. The best way to communicate effectively when there is conflict is to be an active listener and then respond appropriately.

- Do not be afraid to speak up. It's ok to be the one who voices concerns or difficulties. Whether it be in an organization, business, or personal life, be sure to be respectful in your approach and explain yourself in a way that's understandable and to the point without emotion. Be sure that you are practicing open and honest communication when doing so.

- Patience during your communications will always give them time to communicate their issues as well. I spoke earlier about being an active listener as if you are working in customer service. Remaining focused on what someone is trying to communicate will show them that you are, indeed, open to assisting with their issues without emotion. Communication lines tend to break down when there is impatience. Since you cannot control the other side, do yourself a favor and take a breath. The conversation you're involved in is important. If you are confused about what someone is requesting, then repeat back to him or her what you think they said and ask if that is correct. Often this will inspire the speaker to be more in-depth about their needs, which will help you to understand them fully. Take this advice seriously. It can really determine how you interpret a conversation.

- Practicing Effective Communication Skills helps build an effective network as you to become an effective leader whether it is positive or negative. If someone in your network has communicated a need or an issue to you, then your main priority should be to aid him or her in repairing the problem. Following up on an issue is the only way to convince others that you have listened to them and that their problems or issues are important to you, as well. Practicing strong follow-up will also leave the impression that you are involved in the bigger picture. When people see this commitment, they will know you are helpful to include on future communications. This creates a loyal and discerning network that cultivates positive movement forward through communication. This will develop a strong mutual sense of confidence with those with whom you communicate.

Networking Quotes from college graduates who gained success in their fields through networking and communication

"I believe networking is imperative to a person's health, wealth, and success in life. "Your network is your net worth!" The ability to connect with like-minded individuals on positive paths of interest is incredibly valuable. Networking immerses you into cultivating opportunities. Many people are capable of many things, but being afforded opportunities is key. Allow for diversified networking as doing so across multiple facets of life and industry bring about value add that one can leverage forever. I'm a living testament exemplifying how being courageous enough to network with local community, high school students and faculty, college students and faculty, industry recruiters, professional peers and champions, spiritual advisors, financial advisors, and life mentors can propel you above your circumstances and beyond your dreams."

-Derrick Taylor Federal Public Sector Manager, and Community Activist

"It's often stated that " your network is your net worth. While that statement is true, it's often understated how important those who you connect with are in your life, and especially college. It's not JUST about who you are "friends" with. It's also about who you have taken time to connect with, who you have helped achieve personal, educational, and professional goals.

The late great Zig Ziglar said, "You can have everything in life you want, if you will just help other people get what they want."

Those people that you help become your network. They (hopefully) will remember what you have done and will see you as valuable in your life. They will also take a personal vested interest (no matter how big or small) in your success. And THAT'S what networking is all about: seeing who you can help. Not solely because they can help you later; because we should have a desire to serve anyway, but knowing that you will reap what you sow.

Also, when it comes to networking, you want to find people with similar "end game" goals as you. You both want the same positive results in whatever you decide to collaborate on. For instance, as a Student Leader at Hampton University, we were and extension of the Office of Student Activities. Those of us where were very active in the program came together often for common goals. We had a similar outlook on how things should be at our school, and we all used our skills to make them happen. This type of coalition building is not only good in school, it's also paramount for success in the world.

When it came to being a student leader, I think the BIGGEST lesson I learned was, to make the job the master facilitator as easy as possible. It made me somewhat indispensable. Not that I was irreplaceable, because I could be replaced. But what I did became such an integral part of the organization, that if I wasn't there, there HAD to be someone to do my job because my #1 goal was to make it easier on the master facilitator. While I had personal goals, when I was present in the Student Leadership program. The principles in John C. Maxwell's book "360 degree

Leader" leading from the bottom and leading from the middle really come in hand in many organizations"

-Carl Gray III, Entrepreneur

"Great leadership isn't about control. It's about empowering people."-Unknown

High School Community Service Organizations and Their Owners

KARMIA BERRY, FOUNDER OF IAMCULTURED

Karmia Berry, Founder and Executive Director of I AM C.U.L.T.U.R.E.D. has traveled extensively visiting countries within Africa, Asia, Europe, South America, Australia, New Zealand and the Caribbean. A New York native, Karmia created an opportunity to globally enhance the learning experiences for inner-city youth at little-to-no cost to them, exposing them to world travel and encouraging them to create cultural experiences of their own. In just two year from its inception, I AM C.U.L.T.U.R.E.D. has an active roster of student traveler participants embracing their community culture and collecting passport stamps.

Karmia Berry obtained her Bachelor of Arts in Psychology from Hampton University and her Masters of Arts in Marriage and Family Therapy from Hofstra University. She is an active member of Alpha Kappa Alpha Sorority, Incorporated.

I AM C.U.L.T.U.R.E.D., Inc. is a registered 501(c)(3) nonprofit organization, promoting self-

Empowerment and an appreciation for cultural richness and diversity by creating innovative global leaders of tomorrow to envision a life beyond their immediate communities while fulfilling personal and professional goals towards success. We aim to reduce hate and discrimination by redefining social norms through cultural immersion, education and discovery of what it means to be C. U. L. T. U. R. E. D. (Confident. Unique. Leading. Tenacious. Unstoppable. Regal. Educated. Daring) I AM C.U.L.T.U.R.E.D., utilizes mentorship, tourism, empowerment workshops and community service as tools to inspire and challenge students socially, intellectually and psychologically. Providing resources and bringing the community culture to life, we offer workshops throughout the school year in Youth Empowerment, Financial Literacy, College & Career Readiness and The Arts.

Why High School Students? Why Travel?

By the end of 10th grade, a student has completed their adjustment year and are now preparing for college preparatory courses, testing, as well as shaping their curriculum vitae. Traveling the world can inspire ideas, be a stress reliever and strengthen personal identity.

Cultural Series Program

The student traveler and their guardians participate in (5) five world travel preparatory workshops, prior to the students' departure. The workshops are mandatory and are designed to build engagement between the student traveler, IAC Ambassadors and chaperone. The student traveler is responsible for completing assignments and journaling throughout this globally enhanced learning experience.

- IAC Summer Cultural Series Program Benefits

- Obtain a passport
- School-based and community fundraising and service opportunities
- Five empowerment & world travel preparatory workshops
- Week-long excursion to another country
- College prep and mentorship program
- Small travel groups
- College scholarship
- Once-in-a-lifetime memories with lifelong friends
- Community Culture

https://www.iamcultured.org

DOMINIQUE WILKINS, CO FOUNDER OF SHECHICAGO

Since leaving Hampton, Dominique Wilkins has worked 8 years in Finance, Business to Business sales, and as a Leading Consultant in the Beauty Industry before embarking upon her journey in education in 2015. Domonique's love for the beauty industry and entrepreneurial spirit began as a young girl, and has allowed her to become a beauty influencer whose impact is nationwide. Holding strong to the motto that "when you look good, you feel good," she has been able to help women enhance their public images and build healthy self-esteem through proper self-care.

As a mother of two beautiful daughters, Makeup Artist, and Music Educator on the Southside of Chicago, Dominique has been blessed with a heart for people. That heart extends to the work that she does as a co-founder of SHE. Helping young women to channel their strength, humility and be empowered through a focus on Health and Beauty is a direct reflection of the calling on her life, and she is eternally grateful for the opportunity to serve.

SHE began as a conversation between Dominicca Troi Washington and Dominique Natasha, two teachers at a high school in Chicago's South Shore Community, while on a summer road trip to Detroit. The pair shared their life stories with one another, and spoke about their passion for urban youth, particularly young women.

While discussing the possibility of starting a young women's club for their school, both agreed that the name "young women's club" did not fully embody what they wanted to give to the girls they worked with. During their brainstorming session, Dominique turned to Dominicca and said "What about SHE?" The name was a perfect fit, but it was important to both women that it had meaning as well, so the discussion continued. Dominicca suggested the name be an acronym which prompted discussion around what defines a whole woman, better yet, a whole human. It didn't take long for the two to agree that SHE simply means to be Strong, Humble, and Empowered. Excited about what was to come, Dominicca committed herself to developing a strand focused on building the Social and Self Awareness of female youth, while Domonique committed to developing a strand focused on building the image and self-esteem of female youth through Health and Beauty.

Upon the start of the school year, as the program began to gain momentum, Dominicca realized that SHE was missing a key component. The curriculum needed a focus area that would culminate the girls' experiences with both strands, and allow them to put what they learn into practice. After some discussion around the need for a well-rounded curriculum, both agreed that a College and Career Readiness section was needed, and Marrissia Jones, a fellow educator at their school, seemed like an ideal candidate to head this section. The idea was proposed to Marrissia and she agreed to join the team by developing and directing the third and final strand of SHE. SHE's pilot program launched in

September 2017, accepting 44 bright and brilliant young ladies with an overall GPA of 3.7.

http://www.shechicago.org

J. YANCY MERCHANT, JR CREATOR SUCCESS WITHOUT LIMITATIONS

In 2004, through New Face Entertainment, Mr. Merchant put a name to the various community service ventures done as a company called Success Without Limitations. An assortment of college students applied and received financial scholarships. Student organizations such as Fraternities and Sororities receive monetary donations in the thousands. Seminars about suicide and depression were held by SWL. Campus beautification projects were planned and executed like the repaving of basketball courts on the campus of Hampton University. SWL also sponsored various youth sports teams, donated to battered women's shelters, and participated in food drives for less fortunate families. In 2007, as a graduate student, James Yancy Merchant along with undergraduate students on the campus of Old Dominion University created the student organization SWL (Success Without Limitations) which is still active today with over 200 members.

The purpose of SWL is to create a culturally friendly environment through educational, social, and community programming, which will develop leadership and civility among our members. We will strive to accomplish our purpose though the co-sponsorship of campus events, extensive community service, family oriented projects, and campus beautification. Success Without Limitations will bridge the gap between what is learned in the classroom in college and what is learned outside the classroom such as dealing with anxiety, depression, social gatherings as a young adult, and preparing for the conflicts college students may face. Students will also have the opportunity to gain internships through the organization strong ties to the community and alumni.

Success Without Limitations is looking to expand to high schools and colleges across the country. We want YOU to be a part of the movement.

To start an SWL chapter at your high school or college email SWLINC05@gmail.com

Contact SWL if you are interested in our college tour that takes place every April!

For more information visit:

https://www.newfacemanagement.org/success-without-limitations/

COMMUNITY SERVICE

Community service is defined as voluntary work, intended to be for the common good, usually done as part of an organized scheme. Many dictionaries also define community service as part of how people may avoid jail time when facing punishment for a crime. That is NOT what I mean when I talk about community service. Community service is what society needs; it's how people positively give back to others in need. There are a number of ways to provide community service. Being involved in community service projects can help you decide what you actually want to do for a living.

It is important to find ways to give back to youth as we increase our own knowledge and experience… Being that positive presence in our community is imperative.

MERCHANT'S WORDS OF ADVICE:

Remember that creating positive residual impact can help younger students develop their own plans and reach their goals as they come up behind you. As a high school student mentoring middle school and elementary students is a way of giving back to your community. Colleges also look at how involved you are in the community as well. It is apart of many college applications.

Through my event planning company New Face Entertainment, I put a name to the various community service ventures done as a company called Success Without Limitations. An assortment of college students applied and received financial scholarships. Student organizations such as Fraternities and Sororities receive monetary donations in the thousands. Seminars like suicide and depression were held in the name of SWL. Campus beautification projects were also executed like the repaving of basketball courts on college campuses. SWL (Success Without Limitations) is still active to this day with over 200 members. The campus SWL still has the same mission of giving back to the community through service.

I wanted to create something that has a lasting effect past the time created it. Success without limitations was that for me.

For Karmia Berry, and Dominique Wilkins, it was IAmCultured, and SHEChicago, respectively. We were able to have that impact on the community that will permanently change the lives of our youth. These are the goals you want to have. Even if you don't want to create a new organization, you can be a part of organizations like these and impact a student's life to make them better. That's the purpose, to bring our community to a rise in your own way. It is your duty to serve your community as much as possible.

BE A MENTOR

"Each one teach one"

A mentor is defined as a wise and trusted counselor or teacher or as an influential senior sponsor or supporter. To be a mentor is something that falls under community service but it means so much more. Being a mentor means you could be like a big brother or sister to someone who needs extra support in their lives. Some mentors come to mean more to people than actual family. Imagine being able to guide someone through the most critical points in their lives as college students entering a new environment for the first time. Everything you learned up until this point can steer that person into the right direction so they will be a step ahead. Utilizing your personal experiences along with this book will make the experience of being a mentor that much easier and fulfilling. If you're reading this as an incoming freshman or as a high school senior, be sure to find someone you have like interests with and someone you can look up to point you in the right direction. I have little brothers and sisters that I have mentored for over 15 years and, to this day, I still offer advice; we learn from each other, in fact. A mentorship is when you mentor a person or group of people over a period of time. You never know how a relationship like being a mentor can affect someone or affect you until it happens.

One example of a mentor is "This is you go to college" documentary participant, Matthew White who works for the University he graduated from. Matt has been a great mentor for students coming after him. As an educator and administrator, he makes a huge difference in the lives of others by just talking and allowing them to learn from his past experiences. Matt is the director of University relations, serving as Hampton University's spokesperson and is the lead of administrative announcements, breaking news and press queries. He may not realize it but to be alumni and work for the same school means a lot to students, especially for those who develop a love for the university and those who are interested in being in education themselves.

Many of the organizations I have been a part of have a deep mentorship foundation. It is common for student leadership programs, the Greek organizations, and success without limitations to have mentoring or leadership requirements. They are all deeply vested in mentorship. As a high school student, you can be a mentor to younger teens and middle school students. As I stated earlier, "Each one teach one," you can be a mentor and also can be mentored by someone you look up to and can steer you in the right direction.

INSPIRATIONAL PERSON
Justin Sharpe

Justin Sharpe is a Business Management Major at Hampton University from Baltimore, MD. Justin has been a professional photographer and videographer since the age of 16. He first began learning his craft in high school by way of a digital photography course.

As the course went on his teacher expressed that he saw "raw talent" in Justin, and that if he let him teach him, he could be something really special and make some money. Justin first started shooting his high school's basketball games, then candid photos around school. Soon thereafter, prom send offs, senior portraits, and graduation parties became regular gigs.

As more exposure came and he began to perfect his craft, he took over his high schools year book and made major changes. Also he became head of his school's twitter account because of his knowledge of social media marketing and branding. Now at 21 years old, Justin is very experienced in his craft and has worked with teams of 4-5 all the way down to working big parties alone. Some of his best work is his studio fashion photography work.

Events are one of his favorite subject matters to shoot because of the ease of interaction with people. Justin also has a passion for fashion consulting and is looking to pursue personal shopping as a new venture.

If you're looking to see some of Justin's work check out his Instagram @juscobar and contact him at justin_sharpe@yahoo.gmail.com

MENTAL HEALTH

I would be doing everyone a disservice by writing a series of books and not bring awareness to this topic. We have an obligation as a society to protect each other. Suicide and depression are issues that we really don't like to discuss. As an African American male, mental health is rarely talked about because it's often frowned upon to discuss our feelings because we don't want to seem emotional or "soft," These topics have been something I have always brought to light since I was in high school. I used to do community service at the Jamaica Youth Mediation Corps in Jamaica, Queens. One informational seminar/ play we performed was about young black male suicide and depression. Because of the potential positive impact on the community, I took the play to college with me. In addition, I was able to put on annual events on the topic of depression and suicide; we would give out the latest statistics and educate people about the signs of suicidal and depression behavior. We would do skits in which a student committed suicide because the signs were ignored and then put on a skit where the signs were acknowledged and suicide was prevented. I also used my student organization Success Without Limitations as a platform for awareness, sponsoring annual seminars. Now, with social media the epidemic is even worse in our youth.

According to the centers for disease control and prevention

(https://www.cdc.gov/mmwr/volumes/66/wr/mm6630a6.htm)

High School can be very challenging. Someone reading this may be going through something or may know someone who is going through any of these problems. Stress is a very real ordeal. According to the National Association of School Psychologists, stress is the way our body responds to the demands made upon it by our environment and our relationships. In teenagers that can be changing schools, moving, too much school work, divorce, pressure from home, bullying. Pretty much everything a teenager may go through can lead to good or bad stress. Bad stress over a long period of time can lead to more problems that can lead to mental and physical health issues like depression for example.

Depression is defined as a strong mood of sadness, discouragement, and hopelessness that lasts for a long period of time (weeks, months even years)

The odds of adolescents suffering from clinical depression grew by 37 percent between 2005 and 2014, according to a study by Ramin Mojtabai, a professor at Johns Hopkins Bloomberg School of Public Health. The National Institute of Mental Health estimates that 3 million adolescents ages 12 to 17 have had at least one major depressive episode in the past year. Teen depression appears to be on the rise equally among urban, rural, and suburban populations. Research also shows that more dangerous behaviors, like self-harm, are increasing. Depression is the biggest risk factor for suicide in youth. Other risk factors include:

- substance abuse
- a family history of depression and mental illness
- a prior suicide attempt
- stressful life events
- access to guns
- exposure to other students who have died as a result of suicide
- self-harming behaviors such as burning or cutting
- Anxiety

Anxiety is a natural reaction to stress but when it becomes excessive it can disrupt a child's ability to function on a daily basis. There are different examples of anxiety such as obsessive compulsive disorder (OCD), Post-Traumatic Stress Disorder (PTSD, General Anxiety Disorder but I want to just focus on social phobia for the moment. Social Phobia in teens is having a strong fear of being judged by others or of being embarrassed. This affects the positive social interaction teenagers need to have at this age. In today's society, we have to address social media as well. Throughout this book I have promoted and suggested the use of social media and the internet in a positive way and I want everyone to use it for that purpose.

Social media has its positives but can also be abused by overuse and glorifying people you see. Keep in mind that social media rarely shows an individual's failures and down times. People rarely show the struggles and what it takes to get to where they are. Other people post lies. With everything I have mentioned in this book, do your research. It's nothing wrong with admiring and aspiring to be like some people on social media but make sure those people are positive influences in your life and are real.

Social media can also lead to bullying and cyberbullying which usually anonymously sending mean-spirited messages electronically. Sending mean text messages and threats through phones, social media posts creating fake web pages and profiles are examples of cyberbullying according to the Substance Abuse and Mental Health Services Administration (SAMHSA). Students who are being cyber-bullied are often bullied in person as well.

Warning signs of teens dealing with stress, bullying, anxiety and depression:

- Abandoning long-time friendships for a new set of friends
- Expressing strong hostility toward family members
- Experimenting with drugs and/or alcohol
- Cutting or self-destructive behavior
- Acting unusually impulsive
- Forgoing homework assignments

- Skipping school
- Sleeping excessive hours
- Loss of appetite or binge eating
- Risky behavior such as alcohol and/or drugs
- Sexual promiscuity
- Low self esteem
- thoughts/expression of suicide

Everything mentioned above can lead to the worst case scenario that no one wants...suicide.

The suicide rate for males aged 15–19 years increased from 12.0 to 18.1 per 100,000 population from 1975 to 1990, declined to 10.8 by 2007, and then increased 31% to 14.2 by 2015. The rate in 2015 for males was still lower than the peak rates in the mid-1980s to mid-1990s. Rates for females aged 15–19 were lower than for males aged 15–19 but followed a similar pattern during 1975–2007 (increasing from 2.9 to 3.7 from 1975 to 1990, followed by a decline from 1990 to 2007). The rates for females then doubled from 2007 to 2015 (from 2.4 to 5.1). The rate in 2015 was the highest for females for the 1975–2015 period.

According to the Johns Hopkins review in 2017:

(https://www.johnshopkinshealthreview.com/issues/fall-winter-2017/articles/the-rise-of-teen-depression)

Dr. Byron McClure, an intern for my company as an undergrad, is now a part of the National Association of School Psychologists (NASP). Its purpose is to increase the amount of students exposed to the field of School Psychology. The primary initiative was to target undergrad students at HBCUs. It grew to all universities and high schools. By exposing and bringing awareness of school psychology to high school students, NASP increases the number of students who consider entering the field.

In 2018 the NASP had a national conference with over 5000 psychologists from across the nation convene in Atlanta presenting at Morehouse, Spelman, and CAU.

Overall we present to high school students and undergrads about school psychology (who we are, what we do, career paths, how we help people, the importance of mental health, etc.) to create exposure to the field and try to put a focus on attending HBCUs.

~NASP

Below is the link for more information on NASP and its initiative.

https://www.nasponline.org/resources-and-publications/resources/diversity/cultural-competence/multicultural-affairs-committee/nasp-exposure-project-(nasp-ep)

From working with youth in the community center in Queens then doing my own seminars and plays on Suicide prevention are some steps that we created to help prevent a potential suicide. Here are some tips that we put together about suicide prevention when we were developing our seminars through New Face Entertainment.

STEPS TO PREVENTING A POTENTIAL SUICIDE

1. No secrets. If you feel someone is showing signs of suicidal behavior, be honest and open and try your best to get the person to be honest and open. When in college and in life I feel you meet people for a reason. People come and go in your life and sometimes you wonder why. Circumstance may not just be by chance or coincidence. You may be put in someone's life to be that voice they need to hear or that ear they needed to listen.

2. Take any sign seriously. This is a very important step when you are worried that someone is thinking about suicide. If you truly care for the person and don't want to see any harm done to them make sure you take everything they say and do serious. If you see a person with wounds to their wrists that look like they tried to cut themselves, talk to them about it. Don't play around like it is a joke, seem as if you don't care when you really do inside.

3. Listen. Once the person starts to talk, listen. This step is straightforward but very important. Some people just need that person to hear what they have to say about what's going on in their life. Remember the active listening skills we've talked about. Be that person that can provide that open ear that they need to take on life longer.

4. Ask about thoughts of having suicide you don't know how many times I asked this question and it changed the whole conversation and actually HELPED! Asking someone if they are thinking about committing suicide or asking someone straight up are they going to kill himself opens the door for a conversation that will actually STOP someone from doing it. Being straight up and honest really works!

5. Don't leave a suicidal person alone once you get to the point that you know something is wrong and that person is going to try to kill themselves, do not leave them alone. Sit talk and enjoy each other's company. Talk about things that are worth living for after listening to what is going on and what the person wants to talk about.

6. Urge professional help. I'm not a psychologist. I have never acted like one and neither should you unless you are one. At this point, you should make sure you insist on professional help. We discuss the topic in our community the more professional help won't be something that is frowned upon. Many insurance plans will cover at least some of the cost. Dr. Howard Crumpton is someone you can reach out to be pointed in the right direction but I would suggest someone you are close with or your school counseling center.

7. From crisis to recovery below is a list of resources for those who need it. On a personal level, you don't realize how big a role friends and family play in this step.

Support begins at home with family and friends. We have to always support each other and be aware of what is going on in our homes and with our family and friends. I am talking to everyone reading this. Teens, adults, college students, parents and mentors have accountability for the people in your network. Be an open ear. Talk about and look for various warning signs. Be a positive influence on our youth and support one another. If you have personal things going on and this touched home for you, talk to someone. Don't hold it in. There is nothing wrong with talking about things that are uncomfortable.

- Talk about social media and websites.
- Ask questions about what posts are seen.
- Discuss feelings about anything
- Talk about depression and anxiety
- Talk about bullies online and in person
- If something doesn't seem right, address it

RESOURCES FOR HELP:

For information on suicidal and behavior similar to depression reach out to or contact us at www.newfacemanagement.org

www.stopcyberbullying.org

www.connectwithkids.com

www.parentingteens.com

www.kidshealth.org Nemours Kids Health

www.yellowribbon.org light for life program

www.nmha.org national mental health association

www.teenhealthcare.org free and confidential 212-423-3000 Mount Sinai adolescent health center

https://www.washingtonpost.com/news/to-your-health/wp/2018/06/07/u-s-suicide-rates-rise-sharply-across-the-country-new-report-shows/?noredirect=on&utm_term=.f7d0def42bf1

https://www.usatoday.com/story/news/politics/2018/03/19/teen-suicide-soaring-do-spotty-mental-health-and-addiction-treatment-share-blame/428148002/

http://therapyforblackgirls.com

BELOW ARE QUESTIONS TO HELP YOU ALONG YOUR JOURNEY

BY Deon Haraway : Intern with New Face Management, LLC 5 year MBA student at Hampton University

"I hope you soaked up as much as possible from this book because it will benefit you in the long run and will help you reach your goals you've already set! Please answer the following questions to ensure you understand everything you need to know before you go to college"

What are three ways you can pay for college before you graduate?

How do you sign up for the FAFSA?

Based off of your home financial situations which will be the best avenue for you and your family to pay for college and why?

When is the best time to start applying for college?

What programs can you join while in high school can help you stand out to colleges in their application process?

How many scholarships should you apply to while in high school?

What three questions should you ask yourself when picking the schools you want to apply to?

What are the 4 tips that will help you stay on track and make sure you make the right decisions in college?

Provide a short answer for the following questions:

What do you want to do after college?

What is your plan?

What goal do you want to reach in college before you reach your ultimate goal?

SCHOLARSHIP ESSAY PRACTICE

Directions: Below are five sample essay writing prompts. In the space below respond to the sample prompts in detail. Be sure to use appropriate grammar and punctuation.

1. What do you expect to gain from earning a college degree?

_____
_____
_____
_____
_____
_____

2. Write a short essay that describes areas in your life where you showed leadership and overcame an obstacle.

_____
_____
_____
_____
_____
_____

3. Where do you see yourself in 10 years?

_____
_____
_____

4. How would you handle the current issue of gun control?

5. How do you define success?

THIS IS FAR FROM OVER ...

This is how you prepare for college

is College Preparatory for the 4 part THIS IS WHY book series

Be sure to read **THIS IS WHY YOU GO TO COLLEGE**: How to successfully graduate in REAL LIFE Studies Outside the classroom... and beyond

It's available now on amazon and on my website
www.thisiswhydoc.com

Email your success stories along the way as you utilize my New Face Method for success yancy@newfacemanagement.org I want to hear from you every step of the way!!

Part 3 **THIS IS WHY YOU NETWORK** which will go deeper into the "Power of Networking and commutation" through the history of New Face.&

Part 4 **THIS IS WHY YOU GRADUATE** will focus on using the skills you learned through my method outside of the classroom now *after* graduation showing how life is truly a business.

Coming soon!

SUGGESTED READING MATERIAL AND REFERENCES

This is why you go to college, by J. Yancy Merchant Jr

7 Habits of Highly Effective People, by Stephen Covey

Think and Grow Rich by Napoleon Hill

MC Means Move the Class, by Shaundau Woodly, Ph.D.

The Secret, by Rhonda Byrne

Last of the Redmen, by Bill Mitaritonna

Engaging Children in Learning: The Extracurricular Academics Model, by Dotteanna K. Garlington, Ed.D.

History of the Black Dollar, by Angel Rich

Mixed Emotions, by Andrew Nguyen and Pauleanna Reid

SOL Affirmations: A Tool Kit for Reflection and Manifesting the Light Within, by Karega Bailey

You Got Into Where? How I Received Admission and Scholarships to the Nation's Top Universities, by Joi Wade

Guide me to college: 10 vital steps every urban youth need for college, by Starr Essence

https://www.usnews.com/education/best-colleges/paying-for-college/slideshows/10-ways-parents-should-plan-for-college-financially

https://www.forbes.com/sites/susanadams/2018/09/20/rice-university-will-offer-free-tuition-to-families-earning-less-than-130000/

https://psychologybenefits.org/2018/06/29/depression-in-black-boys-begins-earlier-than-you-think/

www.setandachievefoundation.org

@setandachievefoundation Jacksonville, FL offering support and resources to grade school students to inspire them to attend HBCUs

ADDITIONAL INFORMATION:

For teenagers 15-18, **Planet Fitness** is giving out free membership for the summer across the U.S:

"Beginning May 15 through Sept. 1, high school students between the ages of 15 and 18 can work out as much as they want at all 1,700 + locations throughout the US and Canada, as part of the 'Teen Summer Challenge Scholarship Sweepstakes."

All they must do is visit any Planet Fitness locations with their parent or legal guardian and register for free promotion.

In addition to the challenge, the company is giving away a total of $30,500 in scholarships. More than 50 teens will be randomly selected to receive a $500 scholarship and one grand prize winner will be randomly selected to receive a $5,000 scholarship."

https://www.mystateline.com/news/planet-fitness-challenge-lets-teens-workout-for-free-all-summer/1949706522

https://www.planetfitness.com

For more information:

Contact your local Planet Fitness and ask about the teen summer challenge

https://static1.squarespace.com/static/5638c88de4b0ad04e240fd6c/t/5cb0d64d971a184855bfe825/1555093176901/PF_TSC_FAQ_r5.pdf

WHY A BOOK SERIES?

Some may be wondering why I even decided to embark on this journey of being an author. In order to explain why I decided to write this book series, we have to go back in time...

I, along with my best friends, Sean Washington, and Dr. Howard Crumpton, started an event planning company called Straight Face/New Face Entertainment during our freshman year in college. Sean and I went to high school together in Long Island, NY and decided to continue our education at the same institution: Hampton University. There we met Howard who was an intelligent, raw, quick-witted sophomore from Oakland, California.

Three young men with no experience, no major backing, led by only our will and ambition, created something that quickly grew to over a hundred members. This growth in membership occurred by the time I became the sole owner in 2005. New Face even offered college internship credit to help students gain meaningful experience, which often lead to other opportunities for employment in related fields. Under my leadership, its members learned about small business management, financial responsibility, leadership, ownership, networking, and much more. This organization, which now has over 200 "alumni" members includes doctors, lawyers, business owners, teachers, world famous DJs, and artists. The relationships, networks, and bonds formed are unmatched. New Face has also given out over $10,000 in scholarships.

I decided in the summer of 2018 to rebrand the event planning company to form New Face Management, LLC. The process started with creating a documentary based on the experiences of prior employees, associates, and interns of the company, along with the successes and failures we experienced over more than fifteen years. The documentary, called THIS IS WHY you go to college, is an examination of college life outside the classroom and beyond. It's an inspirational story illustrating how the things you do in college shape you into the person you will become. I began to travel across the country interviewing over a hundred business partners and friends.

he first phone call I made was to my longtime friend and former New Face Street team member, Sheronda Lawson, Esq. Sheronda graduated from Hampton University (class of 2006) and is currently an entertainment lawyer. She was the lawyer for other former members on the company who have moved on to do great things in their lives, such as DJ Tay James—Justin Bieber's official tour DJ, and Mark Jackson, award winning songwriter and producer. I felt it was an easy decision to hire Sheronda as my lawyer because of our history and her current success. Our connection was key to the early success of my company; I was her "big brother" in college and she supported New Face in its infancy with marketing and promotions. Most colleges have some variation of a big brother/big sister program where upperclassmen serve as mentors to incoming freshman. Mentors help younger students get involved in various organizations and events and get them accustomed to being a college student. Had it not been for the fact that I was a student leader and an owner of my own business at 18 years old, I would have never met Sheronda. The story of New Face Entertainment is a book in itself... stay tuned.

Fast forward to 2018. I was in the middle of filming for my documentary and had reached Hampton University Homecoming. College homecoming is a time for alumni to return to their Alma Mater for special campus events which usually includes the biggest football game of the year. I always look at Homecoming as a big network reunion. It gives you a weekend to reminisce about your college days a chance to see old friends who live all over the world, and time to reconnect with people you haven't seen in a while. Homecoming gives the opportunity every year to network with people to create more opportunity to build business and personal relationships.

Homecoming every year opens opportunities for business connections and potential leads for the future. It's one big network of people that share the experience of having gone to the same college. During Hampton University's Homecoming of 2018, Sheronda and I hosted the first "In the Industry" panel. We had Alumni from different aspects of the entertainment industry giving their perspective on their jobs and offering advice for those interested in going into similar positions. It felt good to be able to still give back to college students and pass on a message through the eyes of multiple graduates. Plus, it provided an opportunity for students and alumni to connect and learn more about what Hampton students do after graduation. An "In the Industry" panel was held to allow students and alumni from 1999-2018 to network and find out what it took to be successful in their respective fields.

Our expectation was for students to be inspired by alumni and consider ways to make the path easier for reaching their personal goals. The event was very successful with great engagement even during a peak time of Homecoming on a rainy day in October. Our panel was diverse with many different perspectives. Students and alumni were able to network and get a better understanding of many things that are often overlooked when talking about the industry.

Justin Sharpe, a college student from Baltimore, MD, provided filming and photography for the event. As a college student himself, he was able to network with people twice his age and gain opportunities with alumni he might have never been able to meet otherwise. That was the point of the seminar.

On the panel, we had Olympic medalists, worldwide DJs, entrepreneurs, business owners, heads of corporate companies, lawyers, etc.

As the function went on, I began to think about how everything was created and why people were in support of the event. It had nothing to do with the degrees everyone had in the room. People barely mentioned what their majors were. The focus was on what they had done to maximize achievement while in college outside the classroom, and how those things affected their current careers. Don't get me wrong-degrees are important and are needed in many endeavors no matter the field of study. The degree is recognized before anything else to get a foot in the door and shows that a candidate is capable of learning. However, there is more worth in what can be learned outside the classroom, which is a degree in itself. Had it not been for the network, the ability to talk to people, and the relationships built over the years in college, people would not have been interested in listening to the panelists. Each of them owed their success-at least in part-to the knowledge they gained outside the classroom.

Following the success of the event, I decided to take time off from working on the documentary to figure out how to illustrate the power in having a network. I wanted to demonstrate the impact of developing the skills of communication, networking, persuasion, and motivation. Of course, not everyone can develop into a master motivator/business owner/people person. THIS IS WHY I decided to write a series of books creating a pathway of success for those looking for the answers to a test we already passed.

Although there is no physical diploma you receive for everything that is done in college outside the classroom, the knowledge and experience you can receive is unmatched. The degree you receive in the classroom will have more worth if you take advantage of everything that college has to offer outside of the classroom.

Few have mastered the art of turning an idea into a function people would want to attend. Even fewer possess the skill to monetize such an event. People need to learn how to develop this skill and create their own. Part of my personal legacy is passing this knowledge down to others. This series begins that important transfer for information. I will follow it up with seminars and tutorials on being successful outside the classroom.

For footage of the event and a list of the panelists, feel to go to my website www.newfacemanagement.org.

ABOUT NEW FACE MANAGEMENT, LLC

New Face Management, LLC is a management consulting company that supports business and organizations by developing a strategy to become successful through networking and proper planning. The mission is to give knowledge on how to expand your network and grow your business providing an exceptional network to college students, alumni, and entrepreneurs bridging the communication gap in our community.

New Face Management, LLC originated from New Face Entertainment, INC. which was an event planning company, formed in 2005 in Hampton Roads , VA first as Straight Face Entertainment. New Face Ent. endeavored to serve college students and organizations across the Hampton Roads area, creating weekly events such as cabarets, dance competitions, student center events, and social gatherings. New Face served as a safe haven for students to enjoy themselves outside of the classroom with events that catered specifically to the needs of college students. The majority of New FACE's members attended the historically black college (HBCU), Hampton University. This team of student entrepreneurs began with three members in 2001, later expanding to over 100 members in 2005. The entertainment company even offered college internship credit as a means of gaining authentic experience which often lead to future employment in related fields. Under the leadership of its owner, James Yancy Merchant, its members learned about small business management, financial responsibility, leadership, ownership, networking, and much more. This organization, which now has over 200 "alumni" members, includes doctors, lawyers, business owners, teachers, world renowned DJs and artists. The relationships, networks and bonds formed are unmatched.

For more information on the company's services visit:

www.newfacemanagement.org

THIS IS WHY DOCUMENTARY

During the 2006-2007 academic year, footage was recorded of all meetings, events, and social gatherings of the company. The trials and tribulations of balancing academic expectations and a growing business were all documented from hundreds of hours of raw footage. This footage showcases thousands of college students enjoying a pivotal time in their college careers.

In 2018, Mr. Merchant traveled across the country to various states in the U. S. including New York, Virginia, Maryland, Nevada, and California as well as Washington, DC to interview more than a hundred past members about what once was, arguably, the best college event planning company on the East Coast. These interviews were used for a documentary called This is Why: A Historical Reflection of College Life Outside the Classroom. The This is Why documentary will showcase the history and journey of New Face Entertainment over a fifteen-year period and the effect its existence had on the city, its members, supporters, interns, and scholarship recipients.

This documentary inspires our youth in high school to consider college as both a means for continuing to learn and expand one's education and a way of connecting, growing, and making their dreams a reality. We have built a network of over 3 million followers on social media. There was a time when all of these people were together in one city following a collective mission to make college enjoyable and fun. Although we are now scattered across the world as successful adults, the commonality that is

New Face Entertainment still binds us. College is as much about getting a degree as it is about building relationships, stepping out the box, testing the limits of one's abilities, and growing into adults with a unique perspective on life. This documentary will define the WHY in the phrase THIS IS WHY You Go to College.

For more information on the documentary visit

www.thisiswhydoc.com

AFTERWORD

Be humble and grateful to be in the position you are in. My grandmother and my mother always said that there is always someone that would kill to be in the position you are in. Everyday do better. My kids Adrian, LJ, Kaylib and Chloe keep me more motivated than I ever have been to continue to be great in whatever it is I am doing. Find what gives you that motivation and keep pushing. I am here as a mentor to anyone who needs it. Thank you for taking the time to read THIS IS WHY you prepare for college. Now go apply what you learned and be great.

Thank you to all those who took the time to help put this series together. Your input has been invaluable.

First Name	Last Name	Instagram Contact
Andrew	Bisnaught	@babeydrew
Angel	Rich	@angelrich27
Anika	Willams	@nika_denelle
Anwar (DJ SUAVE)	Miles	@djsuave1963
Bianca	Campbell	@binka629
Bill	Mitaritonna	@lastoftheredmen
Blake	Kelly	@blakekelly
Booker	Forte	@bookerforte
Brandon	Taylor	@ayience_fitness
Broadway	Chapman	@pictureb
Bruce	Brown	@brucelbrown0701
Carl	Gray III	@graymatta
Caron	Washington	@kappatalize
Carrington	Carter	@carringtonmcarter
Charles	Stokes	@thediplomat06
Chris	Cardwell	@i_am_goodnews
Chris	Roy	@chris_roy

Christopher	Queen	@frostbyte07
Clay	West	@mrwestmrfresh
Coastal	Ernest	@coach_cos1
Conrad	Llewellyn	@flyfinefocused
Crystal	Neal	@hampton_terps
Danna	Merchant	@dm_merch1040
Day'nah	Cooper-Evans	@iamdaynah
Derrick	Taylor	@custom_taylored
Devin	Green	@officialdevingreen
Dominique	Wilkins	@_domoniquenatasha
Dotti	Garlington	@callmedoctor_18
Dr. Brian	Mcclure,PHD	@bmcclure2
Dr. Byron	Mcclure, Ded	@bmcclure6
Dr. Howard	Crumpton, PhD	n/a
Dr. Shaun	Woodly, PHD	@shaundau
Dr.Timothy	Fraizer, MD	@skilledhands_giftedheart
Edwin	Mcclure	@mygreatcomeback
Ellen	Dunn	n/a
Fresh	Redding	@freshredding

Gavin	McEachin	@young_gav
Ian	Brown	@walt_thizzney
J'vonn	Forbes	@iamjforbes
James	Callaham	@elcapitanambassador
Jayee	Person-Lynn, Esq	@lincolnlawyerla
Jenar	Harrison	@Allaboutdot
Jessica	Gordon-Mckenzie	n/A
Joseph	Walters	@hb1network
Joshua	Estrada	@westmoments
Jovan	Brown	@joaudacity
Justin	Sharpe	@justcobar
Karega	Bailey	@karegabailey
Karmia	Berry	@karmiaberry
Karson	Austin	@kingaustin4
Keion	Mcdaniels	@mymainman_keion
Kellie	Wells	@kelliewellsbrinkley
Khaleel	Artist	@k.artis
Kiira	Harper	@kiiraharper
Laquan	Stewart	n/A
Liad	Onitiri	@kingputon

Mark	Jackson	@markthemogul
Marquis	Dennis	@theartofabs
Marvin	Ganthier	@djmarvalous
Matthew	White	@gingerkid85
Michelle	Rodgers	@michellenicole87
Mimi	Wilson	@nailsbymimi
Monet	Clements	N/A
Mya	Brooks	@flyyfree_myab
Nickolas	Mitchell	@nickluvin4
Nikki	Walker	@imapo3t
Norschon	Sheridan	@thechampagnegang
Paul	Saunders	@passportps
Phil	Smith	@philthedjlp
Rachel	Preston	n/a
Reggie	Morris	@djregyreg
Rev. Mike	Wortham	@michaelswortham
Rob	Rich	@_robrich
Ryan	Marsh	@ryankmarsh
Sean	Gaddy	n/a
Sean	Washington	@seanmwashington
Shante Alesia	Stewart	@shantealesia

Shatera	Smith	@dishea222
Sheronda	Lawson, Esq	@shaymlawson
Sianni	Caballo	@siannijessica
Stan	Wyatt	@stan_the3rd
Tamra	Sease	@tamsease
Tanya	Simpson	@thedreamgirlbrand
Tatiani	Favors	@tatianifavors
Taylor	James	@djtayjames
Traci	Steele	@tracisteele
Travon	Williams	@travonwlms
Tyrell	Clay	@flavaice_
Tyrique	Taylor	@fynaflo
Victor	Rogers	@ceo_vic357
Vincint	Hancock	@djvince757
Wakita	Taylor	@wakilee
William	Hicks, CPT	@integrityisallyouhave

Made in the USA
Monee, IL
15 January 2021